KEY STAGE
3

· KEY STAGES IN HISTORY ·

# EXPANSION TRADE AND INDUSTRY

## R J Cootes  L E Snellgrove

Nelson

Thomas Nelson and Sons Ltd
Nelson House   Mayfield Road
Walton-on-Thames   Surrey
KT12 5PL   UK

51 York Place
Edinburgh
EH1 3JD   UK

Thomas Nelson (Hong Kong) Ltd
Toppan Building 10/F
22A Westlands Road
Quarry Bay Hong Kong

Thomas Nelson Australia
102 Dodds Street
South Melbourne
Victoria 3205 Australia

Nelson Canada
1120 Birchmount Road
Scarborough   Ontario
MIK 5G4   Canada

© R J Cootes and L E Snellgrove 1993

First published by Thomas Nelson and Sons Ltd 1993

ISBN 0-17-435059-7
NPN 9 8 7 6 5 4 3 2 1

## Acknowledgements

The publishers are grateful to the following for permission to reproduce copyright material. While every effort has been made to trace copyright holders, sometimes this has not been possible. We will be pleased to rectify any omissions at the earliest opportunity.

**Chapter 1**
Source 1, p. 6: Corsham Court; Source 2, p. 6: Corsham Court; Source 3, p. 7: Corsham Court; Source 5, p. 8: Courtauld Institute of Art/Leggatt Brothers; Source 8, p. 9: Billie Love Historical Collection; Source 9, p. 9: Fotomas Index; Source 10, p.10: Mansell Collection; Source 13, p. 11: Reading University Institute of Agricultural History/Museum of English Rural Life; Source 14, p. 12: National Portrait Gallery; Source 15, p. 13: Aerofilms; Source 16, p. 13: Mansell Collection; Source 19, p. 14: British Library.

**Chapter 2**
Source 2, p. 16: Mansell Collection; Source 5, p. 17: National Portrait Gallery; Source 6, p. 18: National Portrait Gallery; Source 7, p.19: National Portrait Gallery; Source 8, p. 19: Mansell Collection; Source 12, p. 22: Peter Newark's American Pictures; Source 14, p. 23: Mary Evans Picture Library; Source 16, p 24: Archiv fur Kunst und Geschichte, Berlin; Source 18, p. 24: *left* The Royal Collection, *right* National Portrait Gallery.

**Chapter 3**
Source 1, p. 26: Fotomas Index; Source 2, p. 27: Fotomas Index; Source 3, p. 27: Science Museum; Source 5, p. 28: Aerofilms; Source 8, p. 29: Mansell Collection; Source 10, p. 30: National Portrait Gallery; Source 12, p. 31: Science Museum; Source 15, p. 33: Ann Ronan Picture Library; Source 16, p. 34: Fotomas Index; Source 18, p. 35: Science Museum; Source 20, p. 35: Mary Evans Picture Library; Source 22, p. 36: Mary Evans Picture Library.

**Chapter 4**
Source 3, p. 39: Hulton-Deutsch Collection; Source 4, p. 39: Mansell Collection; Source 7, p. 40: Mary Evans Picture Library; Source 8, p. 40: Fotomas Index; Source 10, p. 41: Ann Ronan Picture Library; Sources 12 and 13, p. 42: Wellcome Institute Library, London; Source 15, p. 44: Alistair McPherson; Source 17, p. 45: Mary Evans Picture Library; p. 46: Cadbury Brothers Ltd.

**Chapter 5**
Source 1, p. 47: National Portrait Gallery; Source 2, p. 48: Hulton-Deutsch Collection; Source 5, p. 49: Mansell Collection; Source 7, p. 49: Edifile/Lewis; Source 9, p. 50: Fotomas Index; Source 11, p. 51: National Portrait Gallery; Source 14, p. 52: National Portrait Gallery; Source 15, p. 53: Mary Evans Picture Library; Source 17, p. 54: Mary Evans Picture Library; Source 19, p. 55: *left* Mansell Collection, *right* Mary Evans Picture Library.

**Chapter 6**
Source 2, p. 56: Mansell Collection; Sources 3 and 4, p. 57: National Portrait Gallery; Source 5, p. 58: Manchester Public Library; Source 10, p. 60: Pat Molloy; Source 11, p. 61: National Gallery of Ireland; Source 13, p. 62: Royal Archives Windsor Castle © Her Majesty the Queen; Source 14, p. 63: Trades Union Congress Library; Source 15, p. 63; National Portrait Gallery; Source 20, p. 65: Trades Union Congress Library.

**Chapter 7**
Source, 2, p. 67: Mary Evans Picture Library; Source 4, p. 68: Robert Harding Picture Library; Source 5, p. 69: Mansell Collection; Source 7, p. 70: National Railway Museum, York; Source 8, p. 71: Mansell Collection; Source 10, p. 71: National Portrait Gallery; Source 12, p. 72: National Railway Museum, York; Source 14, p. 73: National Railway Museum, York; Source 15, p. 74: Mary Evans Picture Library; Source 16, p. 74: Mansell Collection; Source 18, p. 75: Fotomas Index; Source 19, p. 75: Mary Evans Picture Library; Source 21, p. 76: Mary Evans Picture Library; Source 22, p. 76: Robert Harding Picture Library.

**Chapter 8**
Source 1, p. 78: Mary Evans Picture Library; Source 3, p. 79; Hulton-Deutsch Collection; Source 5, p. 80: Mansell Collection; Source 8, p. 81: Mansell Collection; Source 10, p. 82: Science Museum; Source 12, p. 82: Bridgeman Art Library/Maidstone Museum and Art Gallery; Source 14, p. 83; Mary Evans Picutre Library; Source 16, p. 84: Robert Harding Picture Library; Source 17, p. 84: National Portrait Gallery; Source 19, p. 85: National Motor Museum; Source 21, p. 86: Ann Ronan Picture Library.

**Chapter 9**
Source 1, p. 88: Ann Ronan Picture Library; Source 2, p. 88: Bridgeman Art Library/Birmingham City Museums and Art Gallery; Source 5, p. 90: Bridgeman Art Library/Royal Geographical Society, London; Source 6, p. 91: Peter Newark's Military Pictures; Source 7, p. 91: Bridgeman Art Library/The Queen's Dragoon Guards, Carver Barracks; Source 9, p. 92: Billie Love Historical Collection; Source 11, p. 92: Hulton-Deutsch Collection; Source 13, p. 94: *left* Hulton-Deutsch Collection, *right* Robert Harding Picture Library; Source 16, p. 95: Ann Ronan Picture Library; Source 18, p. 96: National Portrait Gallery.

**Chapter 10**
Source 1, p. 98: Hulton-Deutsch Collection; Source 2, p. 99: Rochdale Pioneers Memorial Museum; Source 4, p. 100: Amalgamated Engineering and Electrical Union; Source 7, p. 101: Illustrated London News; Source 9, p. 101: Mary Evans Picture Library; Source 12, p. 102: Tower Hamlets Borough Council/Bancroft Library; Source 14, p. 103: Mary Evans Picture Library; Source 15, p. 104: Mansell Collection.

**Chapter 11**
Source 1, p. 107: Michael Jenner/Robert Harding Picture Library; Source 2, p. 108: Bridgeman Art Library/Lady Lever Gallery Port Sunlight; Source 7, p. 109: Mrs J M Butler; Source 6, p. 109: British Library Board; Source 8, p. 110: Hulton-Deutsch Collection; Source 9, p. 111: Bridgeman Art Library; Source 12, p. 112: Mary Evans Picture Library; Source 14, p. 113: Mary Evans Picture Library; Source 17, p. 114: Fotomas Index.

**Chapter 12**
Source 2, p. 116: Mansell Collection; Source 4, p. 117: Hulton-Deutsch Collection; Source 6, p. 118: Hulton-Deutsch Collection; Source 7, p. 119: Hulton-Deutsch Collection; Source 10, p. 120: Mansell Collection; Source 12, p. 121: Tate Gallery; Source 15, p. 122: Reece Winstone Esq.; Source 17, p. 123: Girton College, Cambridge; Source 18, p. 124: Mary Evans Picture Library; Source 20, p. 125: Hulton-Deutsch Collection; Source 21, p. 125: Mary Evans Picture Library.

# Preface

This book aims to provide a clear, coherent and interesting account for 13–14 year olds studying the relevant core unit of the National Curriculum. Great care has been taken to avoid elaborate language, complex sentence structures, obscure references and unexplained technical terms. At the same time, we have tried to guard against excessive brevity and over-simplification – common enemies of understanding. To allow adequate scope to explain ideas and concepts, and with Key Stage 3 assessment in mind, the basic text has been giving a generous allocation of space.

Although we have adopted a thematic approach to the content, the twelve chapters fit into a broadly chronological framework. A detailed contents list and comprehensive index provide plenty of signposts through the book. Readers should be encouraged to make use of both. For ease of reference, all the topics in the National Curriculum Orders are highlighted in bold type in the index.

Historical sources – both written and pictorial – are numbered consecutively in each chapter. However, to avoid cluttering the book with too many references, not all sources are keyed into the text. There are textual references to all the written sources, but only to those picture sources which directly support the narrative. The documentary extracts each carry a brief introduction to set them in context and all have been carefully edited and glossed. They have not been paraphrased, however, as we believe this would destroy their period flavour.

The *Assessment Tasks* at the end of each chapter cover all three Attainment Targets in a structured and balanced way, taking account of the double weighting of AT1. Many of the tasks lend themselves to either oral or written assignments. The additional groups of questions in the body of the text are designed to stimulate both general discussion and clarification of historical terms and references. Many of these questions are also directly relevant to the Statements of Attainment.

Thanks are due to John D. Clare for reading the typescript and making many valuable observations. We should also like to thank our wives, Sarah and Jean, for their help, advice and, most of all, their forbearance with the demands of this exacting but immensely stimulating project.

*R.J. Cootes*
*L.E. Snellgrove*

# Contents

# Changes in society and agriculture

In the 1740s a rich Wiltshire gentleman, Paul Methuen, was on the lookout for a large house **(Source 1)**. He did not need extra living space. His aim was to find a suitable home for a collection of paintings and other art treasures that he was due to inherit from his elderly cousin. Well-to-do people in those days liked to show good taste by displaying works of art and fine craftsmanship in their homes. Methuen's search ended in 1745 when he bought Corsham Court **(Source 2)**, near the Wiltshire town of Chippenham.

To enlarge the house and grounds, Methuen employed Lancelot 'Capability' Brown – the best known surveyor and landscape gardener of his day. Brown's nickname came from his remark about one estate that he saw in it 'great capability of improvement'. At Corsham, he designed a lake and planted many trees, shrubs and flowers to create pleasant walks and fine views from the house across open parkland. Inside, he built a magnificent picture gallery **(Source 3)** as part of a new suite of rooms.

## Country gentry and the lower orders

Paul Methuen's family, like many other landowners of the time, had grown rich from trade and manufacturing. His great-grandfather, a vicar's son, had married the daughter of a wealthy cloth merchant and taken over his business. Profits from trade were spent on delicately carved furniture, fine china, silver plate, paintings and sculpture. Above all, money was used to buy land. A family had to own land before it could be accepted in the higher ranks of society. It was the ambition of most successful businessmen to buy country estates and turn themselves into 'gentry' **(Source 4)**.

### SOURCE 1

Portrait of Paul Methuen (1723–95) by Sir Joshua Reynolds, one of the leading English artists of the time and the first president of the Royal Academy (1768).

### SOURCE 2

Corsham Court, from the north (1784), showing the side of the house rebuilt by Paul Methuen. The house he bought had been built in 1582 on the site of a ruined manor house.

One way of going up in the world was to marry into money, as the Methuens found. Advantages could also be gained from becoming a Member of Parliament (MP). This often led to well-paid government jobs and friends in high places. Paul Methuen, his son and grandson were all MPs. The grandson went further. He was given a *peerage* (made Lord Methuen) in 1838 – a title which has passed to his descendants.

Although few families did as well as the Methuens in this period, a good number found opportunities to better themselves and buy land. In many village communities the *squire* (the main landowner) came from a fairly ordinary background, and this often showed in his speech and manners. As a Justice of the Peace (JP), the squire had important powers, including the right to arrest and punish certain lawbreakers.

In most villages there were lesser landowners – known as *yeomen* or *freeholders* – who each possessed a few hectares. However most of those who farmed the land did not actually own it. They were tenant-farmers, renting portions of landlords' estates. Both yeomen and tenant-farmers lived in modest houses of timber, brick or stone, with simple wooden furniture. They could rarely afford curtains or carpets. The same

SOURCE 4

A day spent in an English country house in the late 1700s is here described by a French visitor, Faujas de Saint-Fond.

[At breakfast] we find several tables, covered with tea-kettles, fresh cream, excellent butter, rolls of several kinds, and in the midst of all bouquets of flowers, newspapers and books ... After breakfast, some walk in the parks, others employ themselves in reading or in music, or return to their rooms until half-past four, when ... dinner is ready ... If the poultry be not so juicy as in Paris, one eats here ... delicious fish ... At the dessert ... the mahogany table ... is soon covered with brilliant decanters, filled with the best wines; comfits (preserved fruits) in fine porcelain or crystal vases ... [In the drawing room] the tea is always excellent, but ... coffee is always weak and bitter ... Those who prefer conversation or music remain in the drawing room; others go out for a walk. At ten o'clock supper is served and those who please attend it.

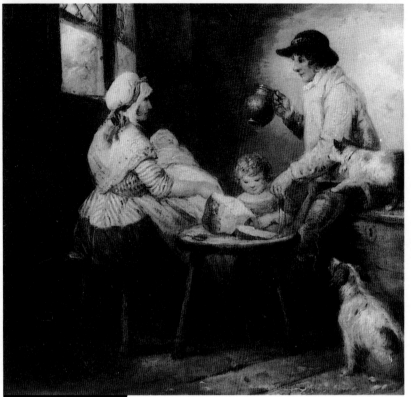

SOURCE 5

English cottagers' lunchtime, painted by George Morland (1763–1804). Such families lived mainly on bread and cheese, with whatever vegetables and fruit they could get. They rarely ate meat.

There is much less about women than men in the recorded history of the eighteenth century. Women were generally treated as inferior and we have little evidence of what they thought and felt. Even well-to-do women rarely had much education and were expected to obey their husbands, produce children and manage the home. Women from poorer families worked alongside their menfolk or became servants in the homes of the wealthy. The whole way of life of the gentry depended upon the work of servants – particularly in the kitchens, laundry, nursery, gardens and stables.

## Rich and poor in the towns

England, Wales and Scotland had a total population of about 7½ million in 1750 – compared with over 55 million today. About a third were town-dwellers. Most towns were very small by modern standards; they were market-places for farm produce and centres where craftsmen worked. London, which dominated national life even more than it does today, was exceptional. Its population was over 600,000 in 1750 and rising fast; fifty years later it was approaching 900,000 (**Source 7**).

was true of village craftsmen, such as the wheelwright, tiler, carpenter and blacksmith.

The great majority of country-dwellers were poor farm labourers or *cottagers* with little or no land. They worked for wages on the larger farms, but were often only employed during busy periods such as harvest-time. In their wooden or mud-walled shacks, often the whole family lived and slept in one room. Poor country folk were generally even worse off in Scotland and Ireland than in England (**Source 6**).

SOURCE 6

Arthur Young, a well-known traveller and writer (see page 13), observed the living conditions of Irish peasants during a tour of Ireland in 1776.

The cottages of the Irish, which are all called cabins, are ... more miserable ... than I had ever seen in England ... They generally consist of only one room: mud kneaded with straw is the common material of the walls ... [They] have only a door, which lets in light instead of a window, and should let the smoke out instead of a chimney ... The furniture [consists] only of a pot for boiling their potatoes, a bit of a table, and one or two broken stools; beds are not found universally, the family lying on straw, equally partook of by cows, calves and pigs.

SOURCE 7

People living at the time realised how quickly London was growing and how busy it had become. Horace Walpole, a writer and former MP, said this in a letter to a friend in 1791.

There will soon be one street from London ... to every village ten miles round! Lord Camden has just let ground at Kentish Town for building fourteen hundred houses – nor do I wonder; London is, I am certain, much fuller than ever I saw it. I have twice this spring been going to stop my coach in Piccadilly, to inquire what was the matter, thinking there was a mob – not at all; it was only passengers.

London in 1751. The river Thames was then an important highway for passenger ferries as well as cargo boats. For centuries, London Bridge (in the centre) provided the only road across the river, but in 1749 a stone bridge was built at Westminster; it can be seen in the distance, on the left.

London was the home of the government. It was also Britain's largest port and manufacturing centre. London received valuable cargoes from all parts of the kingdom and from as far away as India and China. It was a city of contrasts. In wide streets and squares to the west were the homes of rich merchants and the town houses of lords and other wealthy landowners. The poorer classes lived on the east side. Skilled craftsmen supplying the needs of the rich, including jewellers, carriage-builders, tailors, wig- and furniture-makers, could earn a good living. But the poorest, such as dockers and seamen, were often on the edge of starvation.

It is hard for us to imagine the poverty, filth and overcrowding in London's East End. Open sewers in the narrow streets and alleys overflowed with horse-dung, butchers' waste and household garbage. Most of it went into the river Thames, which was also used for drinking water. Not surprisingly, diseases spread rapidly. From records kept by parish churches, it seems that about half the children born in the East End died under the age of five. Violence was as common as disease, since the poor often robbed and murdered to obtain food and other necessities.

Bristol and Liverpool, growing rich on trade with America, had, by the 1750s, overtaken Norwich as the largest towns outside London. Even so, both still had less than 100,000 inhabitants. In Scotland, Glasgow and Edinburgh were about half this size. Places like York, Chester, Exeter and especially Bath **(Source 9)** were fashionable centres where the gentry enjoyed music, plays, parties and balls. However such towns had their poorer areas too where families crowded into rundown cottages, cramped terraces and damp cellars.

The Royal Crescent at Bath, designed in the 1760s. It made the crescent or half-moon shape popular in British architecture. Wealthy visitors came to drink and bathe in the hot spring water at Bath, which was believed to be health-giving. They spent the rest of the time enjoying a busy social life.

## The decline of the 'open field' village

In the mid-1700s at least half the British people got their living from farming (nowadays less than 3 per cent do). The Midlands and South were the most fertile regions. Here many villages still divided their *arable* (ploughed) land into three great hedgeless fields, as they had done since medieval times. Villagers had strips of land scattered about these open fields which they worked like modern allotments. They also kept cattle, pigs, geese and chickens on areas of pasture or wasteland. Such areas were called 'commons' because they were used by all the villagers.

This 'open field' system of farming suited a simple community life where villagers helped each other. For example, families usually ploughed the fields in groups, each contributing a share – perhaps one of the oxen – to the ploughing team. But it was a wasteful, inefficient way of farming. Only two fields were in use at any time – sown with corn crops such as wheat, barley or oats. In rotation, the third field was left *fallow* (unsown) after ploughing to let the goodness return to the soil. This meant the villagers wasted effort ploughing a field that produced nothing. They also wasted time travelling between their scattered strips.

Country folk were slow to give up the old ways; they could usually produce enough to feed themselves, despite the waste of land, time and effort. However times were changing fast. Britain's population began to increase rapidly after 1750, especially in the towns, which relied on surplus food from the countryside. The greater landowners realised they could gain by producing more for sale. With this in mind, they set out to improve their farming methods and get more out of the land.

It was, however, difficult for one or two individuals to do things differently under the open field system without upsetting the farming routines of the whole village. Where open fields still existed, landlords became increasingly anxious to divide

### SOURCE 10

This print, dating from around 1700, shows corn being harvested from strips in open fields outside Cambridge. Each family's strips were scattered around the fields, so good and bad soil was evenly distributed.

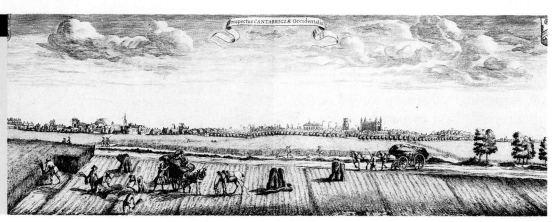

*Prospectus CANTABRIGIÆ Occidentalis*

them up into separate farms, each *enclosed* with hedges or fences. The decline of the open field village, which began long before 1750, was therefore accelerated.

## New farming methods

Much could be gained by cutting out fallow periods and keeping all the arable land in use. Farmers in Holland had found ways of doing this by growing corn and root crops alternately on the same land. Roots, such as turnips and swedes, take their nourishment from the soil at a deeper level than corn crops. So they can be grown straight after corn and still leave the upper soil refreshed for another corn crop next year. Grasses such as clover were also grown in between corn crops as they left richness in the soil.

A few landowners in East Anglia took up these ideas before 1700. But the benefits were not widely known until some years later. One who helped to popularise the new methods was Lord Townshend, a former minister of the Crown turned farmer. In the 1730s, on his estates at Raynham in Norfolk, he used what become known as the 'Norfolk four-course rotation' of turnips, barley or oats, clover and wheat. This was copied by many of his neighbours on the great estates of Norfolk **(Source 11)**. Knowledge of crop rotations then spread all over Britain.

Roots and clover were used as winter feed for cattle and sheep. Previously they had been fed on hay, but there was rarely enough to go round so some animals had to be killed off in the autumn and the meat salted to preserve it. Better winter feeding made this unnecessary. It also helped farmers to breed bigger, healthier livestock and so improve the quality of meat for sale. Enclosed pastures were essential for proper livestock breeding. On village commons different breeds could not be kept apart and diseases were easily spread.

The most famous improver in stock-breeding was Robert Bakewell (1725–95) of Dishley in Leicestershire. He was able

### SOURCE 11

On a tour of eastern England in 1770–71, Arthur Young listed the reasons why Norfolk had become famous for its farming.

Great improvements have been made by means of the following … FIRST by enclosing … SECOND by a spirited use of marl (powdered rock and lime) and clay. THIRD by the introduction of an excellent course (rotation) of crops. FOURTH by the culture (growing) of turnips well hand-hoed. FIFTH by the culture of clover and ray-grass. SIXTH by landlords granting long leases. SEVENTH by the country being divided chiefly into large farms … It will at once be apparent that no small farmers could effect such great things as have been done in Norfolk.

### SOURCE 12

Robert Bakewell's New Leicester sheep. He set out to breed small, short legs and large, broad backs, where there was much valuable meat.

to increase the amount of flesh on the parts of cattle and sheep that fetched the highest prices. Visitors from home and abroad admired Bakewell's feeding methods and the gentle way in which his animals were treated **(Source 13)**. Farmers who copied his ideas found they could breed animals up to two or three times heavier than those on common pastures.

Most early attempts to use machines to improve agriculture were unsuccessful. In the early 1700s, a Berkshire farmer called Jethro Tull invented a horse-drawn seed drill which sowed seeds to a regular

### QUESTIONS

**1** Apart from ploughing, can you suggest any other time in the farming year when families in open field villages would have helped each other?

**2** Why was it easier for the owners of large estates to introduce improved farming methods?

**3** What do you think Robert Bakewell achieved by treating his cattle gently (Source 13)?

**4** Can you think of ways in which the farming changes of this period would have affected the diet of British people?

### SOURCE 13

After visiting Dishley on his tour of 1770–71, Arthur Young had this to say about the achievements of Robert Bakewell.

[His] principle is to gain the beast, whether sheep or cow, that will weigh most in the most valuable joints … The old notion was that where you had much and large bones there was plenty of room to lay flesh on … This … Mr Bakewell has proved to be an utter mistake. He asserts, the smaller the bones, the truer will be the make of the beast … and her weight … will have a larger proportion of valuable meat … The general order in which Mr Bakewell keeps his cattle is pleasing … [He shows] amazing gentleness … All his bulls stand still in the field to be examined … he or his men walk by their side and guide them with the stick wherever they please.

### SOURCE 14

King George III, who reigned from 1760 to 1820, turned part of the royal park at Windsor into an efficient modern farm. His enthusiasm for agricultural improvements earned him the nickname 'Farmer George'.

depth. But nothing came of the idea until improved versions were made, long after Tull's death. A threshing machine – to separate the grain from the husk – was invented in 1788. A further 40 years went by before the first effective reaping (harvesting) machine was produced, in Scotland, by the Reverend Patrick Bell.

Meanwhile, 'improving landlords' continued to popularise new farming methods. One such was Thomas Coke (pronounced Cook) of Holkham in Norfolk. Tenants on his estates were only allowed to use approved crop rotations, and he held agricultural shows at which prizes were awarded for the best new ideas. In 1793 the government set up a Board of Agriculture to promote farming improvements. The Board helped to encourage the growth of clubs and societies where farmers could meet to exchange ideas and information.

### Enclosure and its effects

When land was enclosed, not just the open fields but also the commons were divided into separate farms. It was straightforward if all the landowners of the village were in favour. But often there was disagreement.

squire, the parson and a handful of others usually owned the required amount.

This method of enclosure worked to the advantage of the wealthier landowners. Many smallholders had no documents to prove they owned their land. So their claims were often ignored by the parliamentary officials who came to carry out the Act. Even if they had the necessary papers, many smallholders could not meet the expense of enclosing their land. They sold it instead and worked as labourers for wages. Ownership of land was therefore concentrated in fewer hands. By the end of the eighteenth century, 5000 families owned nearly half the farmland in England.

Enclosure allowed more efficient farming methods to be used. But poorer villagers often suffered, especially through losing the commons. These pastures, where they kept their cows, sheep and other animals, had been almost as valuable to them as their strips of arable land. Arthur Young (**Source 16**), a keen supporter of enclosure, admitted that it brought hardship. 'By nineteen out of twenty enclosure bills the poor are injured', he said. There was usually plenty of work for landless labourers on enclosed farms, but the wages they received were scarcely enough to live on (**Source 17**).

Those with large estates were usually keen to enclose because they stood to gain most from a more businesslike approach to farming. Those with small holdings were often against it. Many feared that they would be unable to farm their land on their own. They were also unhappy about losing their right to use the commons.

Major landowners tried to buy the land of smallholders who were against enclosure. But this could be costly and time-consuming. After 1750, landlords increasingly tried to overcome opposition by getting Parliament to pass a private Enclosure Act. To obtain such an Act, the owners of at least four-fifths of the land had to send a petition to Parliament. The

SOURCE 16

Arthur Young (1741–1820) was the best-known agricultural writer of this period. He travelled widely in Britain and Europe, noting farming improvements, and edited a journal, *The Annals of Agriculture*.

SOURCE 17

In the 1790s a priest from Bath, Rev. Richard Warner, wrote an account of a tour he made through southern England. This is what a farm labourer in Somerset told him.

Time was when these commons enabled the poor man to support his family … Here he could turn out his cow and pony, feed his flock of geese and keep his pig. But the enclosures have deprived him of these advantages. The labourer now has only his 14 pence per day to depend upon and that, Sir, is little enough to keep himself, his wife, and five or six children when bread is 3 pence per pound.

## The relief of the poor

Every parish was required by law to look after its poor people and keep them from starving. To raise the money for this, all houseowners had to pay a local tax called the poor rate, based on the value of their property. In some parishes the poor had to go into a *workhouse*, where they were set to work in return for food, clothing and a roof over their heads. This was called 'indoor relief'. The alternative was to give the poor 'outdoor relief' – a weekly sum of money to help them get by as best they could.

Towards the end of the eighteenth century the numbers in need of poor relief rose alarmingly. Many people living at the time blamed enclosure. There were other reasons too. Partly owing to a run of bad harvests, wheat prices increased by 70 per cent in the years 1780–90 and then more than doubled in the next ten years. Farm labourers' wages did not keep pace with the resulting rise in bread prices. They were forced to beg, steal **(Source 18)** or ask the parish authorities for help.

Something had to be done to support the hundreds of thousands of labouring families existing on starvation wages. In Berkshire, the county magistrates met in May 1795 at Speenhamland, near Newbury, and decided to extend the system of poor relief. In future, labourers would be given money out of the local rates to top up their wages. The amount they received would be linked to the price of bread at the time and the number of children in the family.

This method of making up wages was copied all over southern England and became known as the 'Speenhamland System'. It had very unfortunate effects. Employers refused to give deserved increases in wages because they knew their workers could fall back on outdoor relief. It was deeply damaging to a man's self-respect to work all week only to receive part of his income out of parish charity. The Speenhamland System not only allowed landlords to avoid paying proper wages, it also pushed up the poor rates. The cost of providing poor relief rose so rapidly in the early 1800s that Parliament was forced to change the system (see page 60).

### SOURCE 18

Some of the poor risked their lives poaching game birds or fish on rich men's estates. Potter Macqueen, MP for Bedford, recorded a conversation he had in 1829 with two brothers in Bedford Gaol who were charged with wounding a game-keeper with a gun.

They were two remarkably fine young men … The elder, twenty-eight years of age … replied: 'Sir, I had a pregnant wife, with one infant at her knee, and another at her breast; I was anxious to obtain work, I offered myself in all directions, but without success … I was allowed 7 shillings (35p) a week [poor relief] for all, for which I was expected to work on the roads from light to dark, and to pay three guineas (63 shillings) a year for the hovel which sheltered us.' The other brother, aged twenty-two, unmarried, received 6d. (2½p) a day. These men were hanged at the spring assizes.

### SOURCE 19

English farm labourers drawn in the late-eighteenth century.

# Assessment tasks

## A Knowledge and understanding

1 What were the main differences between town and country life in the eighteenth century, (a) for the poor, and (b) for the rich?

2

| Average weight of livestock at Smithfield Market (London) | | |
| --- | --- | --- |
| | 1710 | 1795 |
| Oxen | 168 kg | 363 kg |
| Calves | 23 kg | 68 kg |
| Sheep | 17 kg | 36 kg |

What changes in farming methods help to explain such figures?

3 Here are some possible reasons for the growing number of poor country folk in England at the end of the eighteenth century:

- Bad harvests leading to high bread prices
- The Speenhamland System of poor relief
- Effects of enclosing the open fields
- The rapidly increasing population
- The low wages paid to farm labourers

Put these in what you consider to be their order of importance and explain your answer.

## B Interpretations and sources

4 Here two twentieth-century historians consider the effects of enclosing the open fields.

Enclosure robbed ... the small farmer ... of the strip that he tilled, of the cow that he kept on the village pasture, of the fuel that he picked up in the woods ... Even if [he] received strict justice in the division of the common fields, his share in the legal costs and the additional expense of fencing his own allotments often overwhelmed him, and he was obliged to sell his property.
(J.L. and Barbara Hammond, 1911)

It has ... been alleged that the results of enclosures fell hardly upon the smallholders ... It is said that the cost of legal charges and of hedging and ditching their new land was more than they could afford ... But they could ... get such good prices for their produce that they could probably afford to pay them, and the cost of enclosing their land has been exaggerated by townsmen who have never planted a thorn-hedge.
(L.W. Cowie, 1967)

a In what ways do these accounts differ?
b Which do you find the more convincing, and why?

5 Look again at Source 8.
a Can you name the tallest building, in the centre of the picture?
b Do you know, or can you find out, when it was built and why?
c What evidence is there to suggest that this was a more religious age than our own?
d What would many of the buildings along the riverside have been used for?
e At this time no part of London was very far from the river. Can you suggest reasons why?

6 What do Sources 5, 6, 17 and 18 tell you about the way better-off people thought about the poor?

## Government, colonies and trade

Since medieval times, Parliament had been divided into two Houses – the Lords and Commons. Members of the House of Lords – over 200 peers and 26 bishops – were much more powerful in the eighteenth century than they are today. They owed their position to rank and title and represented some of the most powerful families in the land. The 558 members of the House of Commons were elected, but only about one in twenty adults had the right to vote. Britain was far from being a 'democracy' with voting rights for all.

### Parliament and the people

In parliamentary elections today the country is divided into roughly equal portions called *constituencies*, each electing one MP. In the eighteenth century, two MPs were elected for each county (122 in all) and two for each borough that was represented in Parliament (a further 432). Oxford and Cambridge Universities also had two MPs each. The allocation of seats took no account of population size. Towns which had grown up since medieval times had no MPs, while boroughs which had shrunk to tiny villages still retained theirs. Some, such as Old Sarum in Wiltshire and Castle Rising in Norfolk, had no inhabitants at all and were known as 'rotten boroughs' **(Source 1)**.

In the counties, MPs were elected by freeholders owning land worth at least 40 shillings (£2) a year in rent. Voting rights in the boroughs varied. Some gave the

**SOURCE 2**

'The Election' by William Hogarth (1697–1764). Eighteenth-century elections lasted several weeks and were times of drunkenness and disorder.

**SOURCE 1**

Daniel Defoe, the writer, visited Old Sarum in the 1720s and described it as follows.

Old Sarum is a double trench, with a deep ditch … Near this there is one farmhouse, which is all that remains I could see of any town in or near the place … and yet this is called the borough of Old Sarum, and sends two members to Parliament; who those members can justly say they represent would be hard for them to answer.

vote to all male heads of household, others just to owners of particular houses or members of the trade guilds. Altogether there were about 250,000 voters, all of them men. No woman was allowed to vote before 1918.

Voting was not secret, so it was easy to bribe or bully electors **(Source 2)**. A 40-shilling freeholder could rarely afford to annoy a large landowner; a merchant or shopkeeper was unlikely to vote against his best customer. Voters usually expected something from the candidate in return for their support. They 'sold' their vote in one way or another – for a job, a favour or simply a good dinner at the candidate's expense **(Source 3)**.

All MPs were landowners, often with interests in trade or manufacturing. They were not paid for attending Parliament, but usually they gained in other ways (see page 7). Many MPs were picked – and told what to do – by a rich lord who was said to have them 'in his pocket'. In such cases the lord owned enough property to give him control over the majority of voters. Seats of this kind were known as 'pocket boroughs'.

## King, ministers and parties

By 1750, British monarchs had given up day to day control of the government. This was now the responsibility of the *Cabinet* –

### SOURCE 3

The Earl of Cork, writing in the mid-1700s, describes the scene at his house during a parliamentary election.

[At election time] our doors are open to every dirty fellow in the county that is worth forty shillings a year; all my best floors are spoiled by the hobnails of farmers stamping about them; every room is a pig-stye, and the Chinese [wall] paper in the drawing room stinks so abominably of punch and tobacco that it would strike you down to come into it.

### SOURCE 4

In 1783, George III chose as prime minister William Pitt 'the Younger' who was only 24 years old. When the Commons objected to his choice, the King wrote this to Pitt (February 1784).

The whole conduct of the Opposition confirms the opinion I gave very early of its dangerous intentions … If the only two remaining privileges of the Crown are infringed – that of negativing (cancelling) Bills that have passed both Houses of Parliament, or that of naming the Ministers to be employed … I can no longer be of any use to the country, nor … continue [to live] in this island.

the name given to meetings of the king's chief ministers. One of the Cabinet chaired the meetings and reported back to the king. He became known as the first or *'prime' minister*. Nevertheless the king still had an important part to play. His permission was required before a matter could be discussed and nothing became law without his agreement. He could also appoint his own ministers, provided they had the support of Parliament **(Source 4)**.

The kings since 1714 – George I (1714–27) and George II (1727–60) – also ruled the German state of Hanover, where they had been born. They came to the throne with little knowledge of British affairs and so had less influence on the government than previous monarchs.

### SOURCE 5

The House of Commons in 1793. The prime minister, William Pitt 'the Younger,' is speaking.

However George III (1760–1820) was born in England, grew up speaking English and never left the country. He was determined to use his powers and did not want to leave important decisions to his ministers – as he believed his father and grandfather had done.

Members of Parliament were not organised into political parties of the kind we have today. However many MPs called themselves 'Whigs' or 'Tories' to give some indication of their views. The quarrel between the original Whigs and Tories about whether James II should remain king was a thing of the past. But differences and disagreements remained. Tories were still loyal, above all, to the monarchy and Church of England. They drew much of their support from the landowning classes. Whigs had similar loyalties but were more friendly towards Nonconformists in religion. Their support included a good number of merchants, bankers and manufacturers.

## The Seven Years War

Trade with colonies overseas was vital to Britain's growing prosperity. But Britain had rivals. Other European nations – particularly France and her ally, Spain – had colonies and trading posts in Asia, Africa and the Americas. The kings of France, who had total power and ruled without a parliament, were always looking to drive the British out of their trading posts. British merchants, strongly represented in Parliament, were no less keen to challenge their foreign rivals. They were confident that the British navy could beat all comers and pave the way for the capture of more possessions overseas. Consequently Britain was often at war in the eighteenth century.

Britain's greatest successes against France came during the Seven Years War (1756–63). This began badly for the British, who suffered defeats under weak leadership. George II was forced to turn to a man he disliked – William Pitt (later Earl of Chatham). Pitt proved a clever and inspiring war leader. His plan was to keep the French busy fighting in Europe while the British seized French possessions overseas. Pitt had an ally on the Continent – Frederick II of Prussia, the most powerful of the German states. Prussia was already at war with France. Therefore it suited Pitt to give Frederick money and supplies for his army.

Pitt's plan worked well. Prussia defeated not only France but also her allies, Austria and Russia. Meanwhile naval victories gave Britain control of the seas. The first major success came in India, where British and French companies of merchants were competing for favours from the Indian princes. In June 1757, Robert Clive (**Source 7**), commanding troops of the British East India Company, won a great victory at Plassey over France's ally, the Nawab (ruler) of Bengal. Clive's force of 3000 chased an army of 50,000 from the battlefield after the Nawab fled during a thunderstorm; hundreds of Indians were trampled to death by their own war-elephants. Plassey broke French power and laid the foundations for British supremacy in India.

### SOURCE 6

William Pitt, Earl of Chatham (1708–78). Although a successful war leader, he quarrelled with King George II and most of his fellow ministers.

Pitt's greatest triumphs came in 1759 – 'the year of victories'. British fleets ranged far and wide, capturing French islands in the West Indies and launching an all-out attack on French territory in North America. Here French settlers controlled the great plains to the west of Britain's Thirteen Colonies (see map on page 20). But in September 1759 British forces under James Wolfe advanced up the St Lawrence river and captured Quebec, their capital city **(Source 8)**. This led to the collapse of the French empire in North America. The year ended on a high note when British warships chased a French fleet into Quiberon Bay in Brittany and destroyed it during a gale.

The war was eventually ended by the Peace of Paris in 1763. Pitt had already resigned after quarrelling with the Cabinet about the conduct of the war. The new king, George III, and a majority of Parliament thought it had become too expensive. Britain gained the whole of Canada and the disputed territory between the Thirteen Colonies and the Mississippi. She also retained firm control of India. Against Pitt's advice, it was decided not to humiliate France by stripping her of every possession captured during the war. The French were given back their West Indian islands, Dakar in West Africa and fishing rights in Newfoundland.

## The quarrel with the American colonies

During debates in the Commons on the peace treaty, one MP gave a warning about the American colonies. He said now that the colonists no longer needed defending against French forces in Canada, they would be much more likely to try to throw off British rule. He was soon proved right.

The British government and American settlers had very different views about colonies. To the colonists America was their homeland. Apart from a governor and a few officials from Britain, they ruled themselves. The British, however, saw the colonies as a vital part of their trade and industry **(Source 9)**. Colonists supplied goods such as tobacco and cotton that could not be produced in Britain's cool climate. In return, they were expected to buy only goods made in, or supplied by, Britain. There were laws forbidding them to trade with foreign countries. However in practice Americans smuggled in large quantities of foreign goods.

Disputes between Britain and the colonists became serious after the Seven Years War. Now that the French threat had been removed, Americans thought it safe to advance west, into the interior.

SOURCE 7

Robert Clive (1725–74). At the battle of Plassey in 1757 he defeated a French-led force of 50,000 men with an army of less than 3000.

SOURCE 8

General Wolfe's attack on Quebec (1759). The city stands on a steep cliff and was well defended. The British army climbed the cliff by a little known route and defeated the surprised French on the Heights of Abraham outside the city. Wolfe was fatally wounded in the battle.

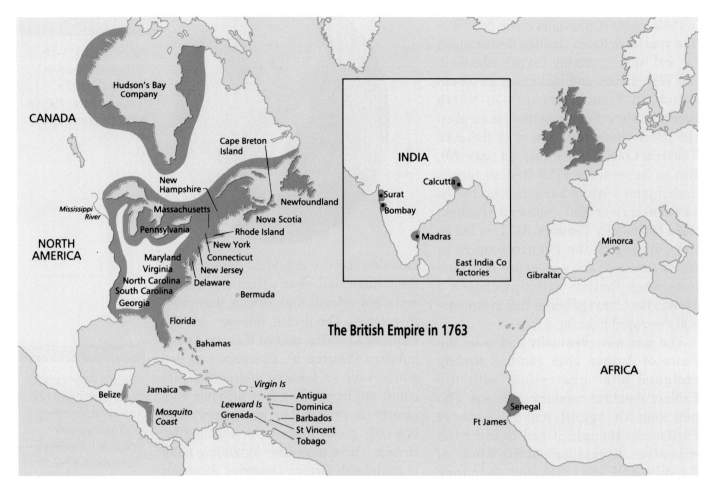

The British Empire in 1763

However George III, worried that this might cause wars with the Indians, issued a proclamation forbidding westward expansion. This was resented by the colonists and many disobeyed it. In 1765 a more serious quarrel arose. Parliament passed a Stamp Act putting a tax on newspapers and legal documents to help pay for the British army stationed in America. The colonists objected, claiming that they could not be taxed by a parliament in which they had no representatives.

Faced with serious riots, the British government cancelled the Stamp Act and replaced it with customs duties on paint, paper, glass and tea. The King, angry that his American subjects had defied him, was against cancelling the Act but his ministers and a majority of MPs got their way. It made little difference. Americans soon showed their dislike of the duties by leaving their houses unpainted, drinking coffee instead of tea and making as many things as possible for themselves, instead of buying from Britain. This hurt British trade, so the government, once again, gave way. It cancelled all duties except that on tea, which was kept simply to maintain its right to tax.

On 16 December 1773, three British ships were boarded by American colonists in Boston harbour, Massachusetts. Disguised as American Indians they threw cargoes of tea overboard as a protest against the British tax (**Source 10**). Britain's reaction was to cancel Massachusetts's charter of self-government, close Boston harbour and demand payment for the tea. This angered Americans who saw the right to run their own affairs, granted by the Crown, as an essential freedom. At a meeting in Philadelphia, Pennsylvania, in 1774 representatives of all but one colony agreed to form an army. A year later, all the Thirteen Colonies went to war with Britain.

## America lost, Australia gained

The American war lasted eight years. It was never popular in Britain. Although the colonists were condemned as rebels, many people thought it unwise to fight such determined opponents so far from home. At first, the King believed he could win because he felt sure most Americans were still loyal to the Crown. But in 1776, the Americans made their famous Declaration of Independence (**Source 11**). After this the French entered the war on the colonists' side, looking to avenge their defeat in the Seven Years War. They sent troops, supplies and advisers to America. Above all, the appearance of French warships at vital moments proved decisive.

In 1781 a British army was trapped at Yorktown, Virginia, by the American general, George Washington (**Source 12**). The British Commander, Lord Cornwallis, expected to be supplied by sea, but when a French fleet appeared he was forced to surrender rather than allow his troops to starve. This defeat ended the war in America, although fighting between Britain and France went on until peace was signed in 1783. By its terms, Britain recognised the Thirteen Colonies as independent states, much to George III's disgust. Five years later, the United States of America was formed.

## QUESTIONS

1 Where were the 'English sugar islands' referred to in Source 9?

2 How would the laws controlling colonial trade have helped to build up the British navy?

3 During the Boston Tea Party, why was care taken to prevent the tea being stolen (Source 10)?

4 Who were the 'savages' referred to in Source 13?

### SOURCE 10

This report of the 'Boston Tea Party' appeared in the *Massachusetts Gazette* six days after the incident.

A number of brave men, dressed in the Indian manner...went to the wharf where the ships lay which had the tea on board, and were followed by hundreds of people to see the event...The Indians boarded Captain Hall's ship, where they hoisted out the chests of tea...[broke open] the chests and emptied the tea overboard...Care was taken to prevent the tea being stolen by the populace...[Next day] the town was very quiet...Those persons from the country returned home with a merry heart...and joy appeared on every face.

### SOURCE 11

This is part of the American Declaration of Independence, 4 July 1776. At the time every American colony had black slaves.

We hold these truths to be self-evident, that all Men are created equal ... with certain rights, that among these are Life, Liberty and the pursuit of Happiness. That to secure these rights Governments are instituted (set up) among Men, deriving their just powers from the consent of the Governed. That whenever any form of Government becomes destructive of these ends (aims), it is the right of the People to alter or abolish it ... The present King of Great Britain has as his object the establishing [of] an absolute tyranny over these States.

George Washington (1732–99), the American commander in the War of Independence. Although not a brilliant general, he was determined, brave and a good organiser.

As Britain lost one empire, she started to gain another. In 1770, Captain James Cook, an English navigator and explorer, charted the coast of New Zealand and landed in Australia to claim it for George III. The loss of America as a place to send convicts meant that Britain's gaols soon became overcrowded. So, in January 1788, six convict ships sailed to Australia and founded a *penal* (punishment) colony at Port Jackson in Sydney Cove (**Source 13**). Before long, free settlers from Britain had begun to colonise both Australia and New Zealand.

## French Revolution and Irish Rebellion

The French government soon had cause to regret helping the American colonists against Britain. The cost of the war increased France's already massive debts and there was growing criticism of the king's extravagance and misrule. In July 1789, the people of Paris rose in revolt, driven to despair by food shortages. The Bastille, a royal prison, was stormed by a mob and the guards killed. The revolutionaries proposed far-reaching reforms, taking as their motto, 'Liberty, Equality, Fraternity (brotherhood)'.

By 1792 France had a revolutionary government and was at war with the emperors of Prussia and Austria, who wanted to crush the revolution. Next year the French executed their king, Louis XVI. All fit men were enlisted in the army which won sweeping victories. Britain was brought into the war in 1793 after French troops occupied Belgium. France had further threatened Britain by offering to help the Irish get rid of British rule in Ireland.

For centuries Britain had mistreated most Irish people because they were Catholics. No Catholic was allowed to take part in politics or hold a government job. During the French Revolution, discontented Irish Catholics formed a Society of United Irishmen (1791) and appealed to the French to help them make Ireland independent. But when the French sent forces they were driven off by bad weather. In 1798 the Irish tried to expel the British without foreign aid. They rose in revolt but were defeated at the battle of Vinegar Hill.

The British prime minister, William Pitt 'the Younger' (son of the Earl of Chatham), realised Britain had been in danger. A French landing in Ireland could have given the enemy a base for attacking Britain. To try to stop this happening in the future, Pitt proposed that Ireland should be united with England, Wales and Scotland. In the resulting Act of Union (1800) Britain and Ireland agreed to share

This letter was written in November 1788 by a woman convict to a friend or relative in England. It describes conditions at Port Jackson, which later grew into the city of Sydney.

Our passage (voyage) was tolerably favourable; but the inconveniences since suffered for want of shelter, bedding etc. are not to be imagined by any stranger ... We have two streets, if four rows of miserable huts ... deserve the name ... Windows they have none so lattices of twigs are made ... The savages continue to do us harm ... I know not how many people they have killed ... As for the distresses of the women, they are past description ... Those who have young children are quite wretched ... Several women became pregnant on the voyage ... [They] are left since by their partners who have returned to England.

the same king, parliament and army; 100 Irish MPs were to sit in the House of Commons and 28 Irish peers and four bishops in the Lords.

Union might have brought peace and prosperity had not George III, a keen Protestant, blocked a vital part of Pitt's plan. This was Catholic Emancipation (freedom) to take part in politics and hold government jobs **(Source 15)**. The Irish had assumed that this would be part of the terms of the union. Without it, they could only be represented by Protestant MPs. This made the Act of Union a fraud so far as Irish Catholics were concerned.

## The Napoleonic Wars

The 1799, Napoleon Bonaparte, the most successful of the French revolutionary generals, seized power in France. Five years later he made himself emperor. Napoleon was a military genius. In a series of remarkable victories he defeated Austria, Prussia and Russia and made himself master of Europe. Only the British navy, defending the Channel, held out against him.

In 1804, Napoleon planned an invasion of England. Hundreds of flat-bottomed boats and 150,000 of his finest troops were assembled on the Channel coast. But a blockade of French ports by the British navy meant his fleet could not escort the

invading force across the Channel. When a French fleet at Toulon escaped into the Mediterranean it was pursued and forced to shelter in the Spanish harbour of Cadiz. Napoleon ordered his commander to go out and fight. On 21 October 1805 his fleet, and the ships of his ally, Spain, were destroyed off Cape Trafalgar by British warships led by Lord Nelson.

Victory at Trafalgar gave Britain command of the seas for the rest of the war. She was able to capture islands in the Mediterranean and West Indies from France and take over the Cape of Good Hope (later South Africa) from Napoleon's Dutch allies. From 1808, the Royal Navy also supplied British troops in Portugal after the Portuguese had rebelled against Napoleon's rule. The British commander, Arthur Wellesley (later Duke of Wellington), fought a series of campaigns which drove the French out of Spain and Portugal (1809–14). He crossed the border into France just before Napoleon

### QUESTIONS

1. Why were the French willing to help the Irish gain their independence of Britain?

2. In the Napoleonic Wars what advantage did Britain get from being an island?

3. Why was a French invasion of Britain unlikely after the battle of Trafalgar?

4. In Source 16, what impression of Lord Nelson does the artist give, and how is this achieved?

### SOURCE 15

George III believed that if he accepted Catholic Emancipation he would break his coronation oath to defend the Church of England. This comes from a letter to Pitt (February 1801).

A sense of religious as well as political duty has made me, from the moment I mounted the throne, consider the ... obligation on me to maintain the Church of England ... Those who hold employment in the State must be members of it, and obliged not only to take oaths against Popery (the Catholic faith) but to receive the Holy Communion agreeably to the rites (ceremonies) of the Church of England.

was overthrown, in March 1814, by the armies of a European alliance.

Napoleon was banished to the island of Elba in the Mediterranean. But in March 1815 he returned to France. Thousands of his soldiers flocked to join him and he advanced into Belgium where troops led by Wellington and the Prussian general, Prince Blücher, were stationed. Napoleon took them by surprise, defeating Blücher and forcing Wellington to retreat. The British took up a defensive position on a ridge outside the village of Waterloo, near Brussels.

On 18 June 1815, Wellington's forces drove off repeated French attacks, with heavy losses. In the afternoon the Prussians arrived **(Source 17)**. Caught between the two armies, Napoleon's forces were destroyed. The victory at Waterloo ended the war. Napoleon was sent to the remote island of St Helena in the Atlantic, where he died in 1821. In the peace settlement of 1815 Malta, Ceylon (now Sri Lanka), the Cape of Good Hope, Mauritius and some West Indian islands were added to the British Empire.

**SOURCE 17**

Captain Gronow of the First Foot Guards tells how, with the Duke of Wellington close at hand, the British repelled a French cavalry charge at Waterloo.

You saw what appeared to be an overwhelming long, moving line which glittered like a stormy wave of the sea … They were the famous [French] soldiers who had fought on most of the battlefields of Europe. In an incredibly short time they were within twenty yards of us … Every man in the [British] front ranks knelt, and a wall bristling with steel, held together by steady hands, presented itself to the enemy. Our well-directed fire brought men and horses down, and before long the utmost confusion arose in their ranks. The Duke sat unmoved … 'The battle is mine,' [he said] 'and if the Prussian arrive soon, there will be an end of the war'.

**SOURCE 18**

A dramatic scene from the battle of Waterloo. Sergeant Ewart of the Scots Greys seizes the battle standard of the French 45th regiment. Below: a wartime portrait of Arthur Wellesley, later Duke of Wellington (1769-1852).

# Assessment tasks

## A Knowledge and understanding

1 **a** In what ways was the system of parliamentary elections described in this chapter corrupt?
   **b** Why do you think it was allowed to continue?

2 Make a timeline of important dates in Britain's wars, between 1756 and 1815. For each of the three major wars, divide your entries into the following columns: (i) land battles or campaigns; (ii) naval battles or expeditions; (iii) gains and losses to the British Empire.

3 **a** Make a list of the causes of the American War of Independence, divided into (i) long-term causes, and (ii) short-term causes.
   **b** Which do you think was the most important single cause, and why?

## B Interpretations and sources

4 Here are two modern views of the Boston Tea Party.

The East India Company was empowered to ship its tea direct to American ports ... [which] would benefit both the East India Company and the American consumer ... This amiable plan failed to reckon with ... [American merchants] whose warehouses were full of smuggled Dutch tea, which they expected to sell at a handsome profit ... An organised gang, childishly disguised as Indian braves, threw the cargo of tea into Boston harbour.
(D.C. Somervell, 1942)

[Americans] argued that if Parliament could give the East India Company a monopoly of trade in tea, it could arrange for monopolising other commodities as well ... Once submit to parliamentary taxation, went the argument, and you lay yourself open to its tyranny over you ... Excellent organisation was revealed when the tea reached America ... In Boston a great protest meeting was followed by the famous tea party.
(H. Bragdon & S. McCutchen, 1969)

One of these books is American, the other British. Which is which and how can you tell?

5 What can be learned from Sources 4 and 15 about George III's attitude towards the monarchy?

6 Look carefully at Source 2.
   **a** Why was this method of voting open to bribery and corruption?
   **b** Can you see any signs of corruption in the picture?
   **c** What seems to be the attitude of the onlookers to the election?
   **d** How does voting today differ from that shown here?

# 'The industrial revolution'

## The beginning of factory production

The main industries in the eighteenth century, apart from farming, were cloth-making and metal manufacturing. Unlike today, work was centred round the home. Whole families, including the children, worked together in cottages and small backyard workshops. They owned their own tools or hand-worked machines, such as hammers and files in the metal trades or spinning wheels and handlooms in cloth-making. After about 1760, however, 'domestic industry' of this kind began to decline. The main reason was the invention of large water-powered and steam-driven machines.

Powered machinery led to large-scale production in *factories* with hundreds of workers. This, in turn, led to the growth of industrial towns. Britain was the first country in the world to experience these changes. Their effect was so great that historians call them a 'revolution' – a word normally used to describe events as dramatic as the overthrow of governments. 'The Industrial Revolution' was a turning point in history – it led to the kind of society we have today.

**SOURCE 1**

Hand-wheel spinning in the days of home-based industry. Short lengths of wool or cotton were joined into a continuous yarn. Spinning was mostly done by young, unmarried women ('spinsters').

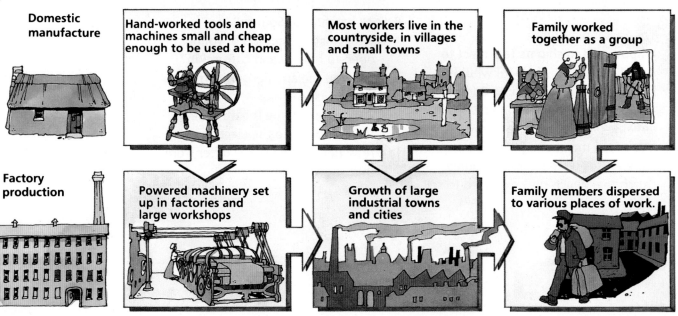

Domestic manufacture

Hand-worked tools and machines small and cheap enough to be used at home

Most workers live in the countryside, in villages and small towns

Family worked together as a group

Factory production

Powered machinery set up in factories and large workshops

Growth of large industrial towns and cities

Family members dispersed to various places of work.

The effect of the Industrial Revolution on the family

## Mills for cotton spinning

Since ancient times, cloth had mostly been made out of wool. However the 'revolution' in textiles began in the cotton industry – and also on a much smaller scale in silk-making (**Source 2**). The cotton industry only started in Britain in the 1600s, using cheap raw cotton from America. It developed rapidly in Lancashire, where the raw material was shipped into the country through the port of Liverpool.

Spinning cotton into yarn by hand was a slow process. Consequently weavers (usually men), who made the cloth, often could not get enough yarn to keep their looms busy. This problem got worse in the mid-1700s, when improvements to the handloom speeded-up weaving. A quicker method of spinning yarn was now even more urgently needed.

Around 1765, James Hargreaves, a carpenter from Blackburn, found an answer with his *spinning jenny* (**Source 3**). This worked like a spinning wheel, except that one worker could spin several threads at once by turning a handle. The earliest jennies did the work of six or eight hand-spinners (**Source 4**). By the time Hargreaves died, in 1778, models with 80 spindles were operating in factories driven by water-wheels. These factories were called *mills* because people were used to seeing water-wheels working flour-mills.

**SOURCE 3**

A copy of James Hargreaves's spinning jenny, in London's Science Museum. Originally it was probably called a 'gin' or 'ginny' – then common words for engine.

**SOURCE 4**

Hand-operated spinning jennies, used in workers' homes, helped to increase the family income. James Ogden, a Manchester teacher, wrote this in 1783.

[Spinning jennies] were first used by the country people … twelve spindles being thought a great affair at first … [although] the awkward posture required to spin on them was discouraging to grown up people … Children, from nine to twelve years of age, [could] manage them with dexterity (skilfully), which brought plenty into families, that were before overburdened with children.

Soon after the invention of the jenny, Richard Arkwright, a wig-maker from Preston, came up with a different kind of spinning machine. Arkwright was not an inventor; he was a clever businessman who profited from the ideas of others. In 1768 he paid a clockmaker to construct a machine called the *water-frame*. It was based on an earlier, unsuccessful machine

## SOURCE 5

Water-wheel once used at Cromford mill.

## SOURCE 6

This advertisement for workers at Arkwright's Cromford mill appeared in *The Derby Mercury* in December 1771. 'Tooth and pinion' refers to cog-wheels fitting into each other.

WANTED immediately, two journeymen clock-makers, or others that understand tooth and pinion well; also a smith that can forge and file. Likewise two wood-turners that have been accustomed to wheel-making, spoke-turning, etc. Weavers residing at the mill may have good work. There is employment at the above place for women, children, etc. and good wages.

## SOURCE 7

The Reverend Edmund Cartwright (1743–1823) here describes how he came to invent his power-loom.

In the summer of 1784, I fell in company with some gentlemen of Manchester, when the conversation turned on Arkwright's spinning machinery. One of the company observed that … so many mills would be erected, and so much cotton spun, that hands never could be found to weave it … I replied that Arkwright must then set his wits to work to invent a weaving mill … [but] the Manchester gentlemen … agreed that the thing was impracticable (could not be done) … Afterwards … it struck me that, as in plain weaving there could only be three movements … there would be little difficulty in producing and repeating them. Full of these ideas, I immediately employed a carpenter and smith to carry them into effect.

from the West Midlands. The water-frame had four pairs of rollers which turned at different speeds to draw out and twist the thread.

Unlike the jenny, the water-frame could not be operated by hand. It needed the power of a water-wheel. So it led to the setting-up of factories. Arkwright opened his first successful mill in 1771, at Cromford, near Derby. Many more followed. The largest, in Lancashire, housed 600 workers. Arkwright showed great energy and business ability in the way he obtained financial backers, organised production and trained his workers (**Source 6**). He was given a knighthood and died a rich man, in 1792.

Yarn from the water-frame was strong but coarse in texture. Jenny-spun yarn was of fine quality but broke easily. In 1779, Samuel Crompton from Bolton combined the best features of the two machines to produce his *spinning mule*. In time, this replaced the other machines. The transfer of cotton-spinning from homes to factories was almost complete by 1800. By then, water-power was giving way to steam (see page 31).

## Further advances in textiles

Previously there had not been enough yarn to keep weavers busy. Now yarn was so plentiful there was more than they could use. Consequently weavers were in great demand and able to earn very high

### QUESTIONS

1. Why were the skills of a clockmaker useful in building textile machines?

2. Why did Arkwright choose the Derbyshire hills for his first factories?

3. A mule is a cross between a donkey and a horse. Why do you think Crompton called his machine a 'mule'?

4. Why were handloom weavers so bitterly opposed to the power loom? Source 8 may help you find an answer.

wages. The industry urgently needed a mechanical loom to speed up weaving. Many inventors tried and failed. In the end the answer was found by a country parson, Edmund Cartwright, who had no technical training **(Source 7)**. Cartwright's first effort, in 1785, was crude and clumsy, but within four years he had produced a workable steam-driven loom.

Handloom weavers, seeing their livelihood threatened, tried to stop the use of power-looms. When Cartwright set up a factory in partnership with a Manchester firm, weavers burned it down. But they were fighting a losing battle. Mass production of cloth brought down prices and so reduced the wages that could be earned on the handloom **(Source 9)**. In 1830, handlooms still outnumbered power-looms in the cotton industry by three to one, but by the 1840s the power-loom was supreme.

The inventions in the cotton industry took an average of 30 years to be applied to woollen cloth-making – partly because wool is more difficult to twist and stretch on a spinning machine. Consequently, by 1800 cotton manufacturing had overtaken wool as Britain's leading industry. Even so, in the villages of West Yorkshire – which was now the main centre of the woollen industry – thousands of 'domestic' cloth workers made a good

A very great number of the weavers are unable to provide for themselves and their families a sufficiency of food of the plainest and cheapest kind. They are clothed in rags, and indisposed (unwilling) on this account to go to any place of worship or to send their children to the Sunday schools. They have scarcely anything like furniture in their houses. Their beds and bedding are of the most wretched description and many of them sleep upon straw.

living. They used jennies and mules for spinning, but these were mainly small, hand-worked versions. The power-loom did not come into general use in the woollen industry until the 1850s.

Businesses were generally much smaller in the woollen industry. An exception was that of Benjamin Gott, the first of the great factory masters in Yorkshire. Gott used powered spinning machines in two large factories he set up in Leeds in the 1790s. His business received a boost when Britain went to war with France in 1793. This resulted in big government contracts for army clothing. So great was the demand for cheap, mass-produced woollen cloth that Gott ran night shifts to keep his machines fully employed.

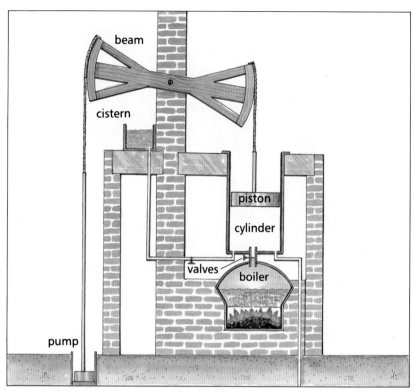

beam

cistern

piston

cylinder

valves

boiler

pump

Thomas Newcomen's steam-atmospheric engine

Steam from the boiler was fed into the cylinder. The piston rose, under the weight of the pump rods, until cold water let in from the cistern caused the steam to condense. A vacuum (absence of air) was created under the piston which caused atmospheric pressure above to force it back to the bottom of the cylinder. The up and down movement of the piston made the beam see-saw and this worked the pump.

## Steam power

The water-wheels that drove the early textile mills needed fast-flowing rivers of the kind found only in hilly regions. Before factories could be set up in low-lying areas, a new form of power would be needed. Steam was the answer. The first practical steam engines were made to pump water. They were invented by Cornishmen trying to stop flooding in the local tin mines.

An engine constructed in 1698 by Thomas Savery, an army officer, was not powerful enough to drain deep mines. It was left to Thomas Newcomen, a blacksmith from Dartmouth, to design a more effective steam engine, in about 1706 (see diagram). After improving on his first, clumsy efforts, Newcomen formed a company in 1711 to build and sell his engines. They were much in demand, not just for tin mines but also in the coalfields. By the 1770s there were 100 Newcomen engines in the Northumberland and Durham coalfield alone.

Glasgow University had a working model of a Newcomen engine for teaching students. In 1763 it was sent for repair to a young scientific instrument-maker called James Watt. Watt was struck by the engine's inefficiency and set out to improve it. He noticed that each time water was injected into the cylinder much of the next intake of steam was wasted in re-heating the cylinder to the necessary 100°C. Watt's solution was to draw the steam out of the cylinder after each upward thrust of the piston and condense it in a separate water-cooled compartment.

Watt's *separate condenser* saved a lot of steam, so less fuel was needed to work the engine. His next improvement (1764) was to fix an airtight cover on the cylinder and inject the steam first on one side of the piston and then on the other. A *valve box* was added for this purpose (see diagram). This invention meant atmospheric pressure was no longer used; the engine was entirely steam-driven.

The first attempt to manufacture Watt's improved steam engine, in 1769, proved a failure. The parts, made by his business

SOURCE 10

James Watt (1736–1819). He was the son of an architect and shipbuilder from Greenock, near Glasgow. Unlike most inventors of his day, Watt had some scientific training.

A Sheffield iron and steel firm, Samuel Walker and Co., enquired about obtaining a Boulton and Watt steam engine in 1781. This is part of Boulton and Watt's reply.

We have had many public trials made between our engine and the common (Newcomen) engine and in some of them ours proved more than four times better, and in none so little as three times better … as we burn but one third of the coal … As our profits arise from the superiority of our engine … [we require] it to be erected according to our plans and directions … for which we ask an annual sum equal to the value of one third of the coals saved.

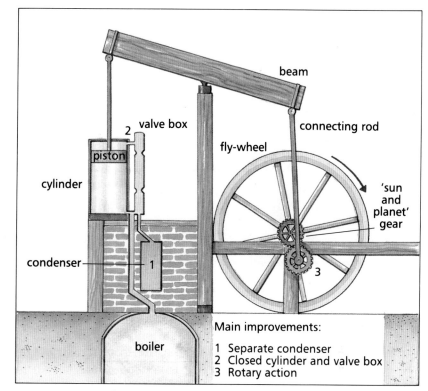

James Watt's rotative steam engine

In this early version of the rotative engine, the connecting rod was geared to the fly-wheel by means of cog-wheels. This 'sun and planet gear' was suggested by William Murdoch, a self-taught Scottish engineer who was foreman at Boulton and Watt's Soho factory, near Birmingham.

partner, John Roebuck, at the Carron ironworks near Falkirk, were not accurate enough. All seemed lost when Roebuck went bankrupt in 1773. However, luckily for Watt, Roebuck's two-thirds share in the partnership was taken over by Matthew Boulton, a hardware manufacturer from Birmingham. Boulton's products were well known for their high quality workmanship. The trial engine was rebuilt successfully and in 1775 Boulton and Watt steam engines began to be delivered to customers (Source 11).

At this stage the engine was still a pump. The real breakthrough was the invention of *rotary motion*, in 1781. Instead of pumping, the beam turned a fly-wheel which could be attached by a belt to various kinds of machinery. 'Rotative engines' were first used to work hammers and rollers in iron-making, and then to power cotton mills. By the early 1800s they were replacing water-wheels in sugar-refining, brewing, flour-milling and many other industries. Large-scale industry now became concentrated in coalfield areas, where fuel for steam-engines was close at hand.

SOURCE 12

This Boulton and Watt rotative steam engine, built in 1788, is in London's Science Museum.

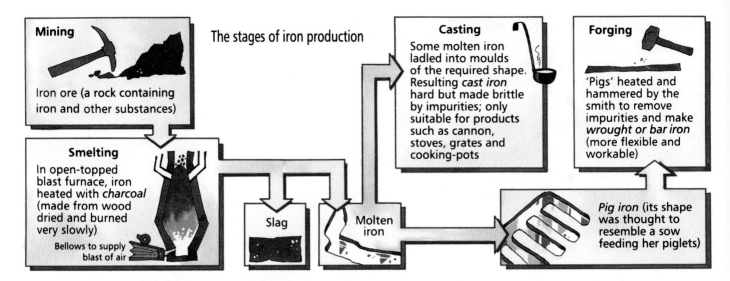

**The stages of iron production**

**Mining**
Iron ore (a rock containing iron and other substances)

**Smelting**
In open-topped blast furnace, iron heated with *charcoal* (made from wood dried and burned very slowly)
Bellows to supply blast of air

Slag

Molten iron

**Casting**
Some molten iron ladled into moulds of the required shape. Resulting *cast iron* hard but made brittle by impurities; only suitable for products such as cannon, stoves, grates and cooking-pots

**Forging**
'Pigs' heated and hammered by the smith to remove impurities and make *wrought or bar iron* (more flexible and workable)

*Pig iron* (its shape was thought to resemble a sow feeding her piglets)

## The mass production of iron

The need for more and more iron to build steam engines and other machines led to great advances in the iron industry. The main stages in iron-making are shown in the diagram. First, iron ore was smelted (melted) in a furnace to separate out the metal. Then the molten iron was either poured into moulds to make *cast iron* goods or run off into channels called 'pigs' in a bed of sand. Lengths of pig-iron were re-heated and hammered by smiths at their forges to remove impurities. The resulting *bar* or *wrought* iron was not as hard as cast iron but much more supple and workable. It was made into tools, nails and all kinds of hardware.

In the early 1700s Britain's iron industry was declining, despite rich deposits of iron-ore. The reason was a severe shortage of timber to make charcoal – the fuel used in blast furnaces. Many iron workings had been abandoned because the woodlands for miles around had been felled. As a result hardware manufacturers were having to import increasing amounts of pig-iron from Sweden and Germany **(Source 13)**.

Countless attempts to solve this problem by using 'pit-coal' instead of charcoal had failed. We now know this was because sulphur in the coal made the pig-iron brittle and unworkable. However Abraham Darby, a Quaker ironmaster from Coalbrookdale in Shropshire, found an answer. Darby (1677–1717) made it possible to use coal for smelting by first turning it into coke. Like charcoal, coke is almost pure carbon. But unlike charcoal it could be produced cheaply in large quantities **(Source 14)**.

### SOURCE 13

Birmingham was already famous for ironmongery, including locks, pins, buttons and nails. Here Lord Shelburne, who went there in 1766, tells how jobs were split up between workers (called *the division of labour*).

Instead of employing the same hand to finish a button or any other thing, they subdivide it into as many different hands as possible, finding beyond doubt that the human faculties, by being confined to a repetition of the same thing become … [quicker] and more to be depended on than when obliged … to pass from one to another … By this means, the work becomes so simple that, five times in six, children of six or eight years old do it as well as men.

### SOURCE 14

Abraham Darby's discovery of coke smelting is described in this letter written by his daughter-in-law, Abiah, in 1775.

About the year 1709 he came into Shropshire to Coalbrookdale … He here cast iron goods in sand out of the blast furnace that blowed with wood charcoal … Sometime after he suggested … [smelting] with pit coal: upon this he first tried with raw coal as it came out of the mines, but it did not answer. He, not discouraged, had the coal coked into cinder as is done for drying malt, and it then succeeded to his satisfaction.

## QUESTIONS

**1** Watt's improvement of the Newcomen engine mattered more in tin mines than coal mines. Can you work out why?

**2** By the early 1800s Britain's iron industry had become established in coalfield areas. Can you explain why?

**3** In Source 16 rabbles are shown in trays of water. What does this tell you about the nature of the work?

**4** Can you suggest a reason why transport by river and sea was important to the development of coal-mining in this period?

### SOURCE 15

Early nineteenth-century painting of the world's first iron bridge – built in 1779 by the third Abraham Darby (1750–91). Made entirely of cast iron, it spans the river Severn at Ironbridge in Shropshire.

Iron from Abraham Darby's coke furnaces was only suitable for casting. It was left to his son, also named Abraham (1711–63), to improve the process. Instead of coking coal in heaps, as his father had done, Abraham Darby II used coking ovens to produce purer coke. And to increase the temperature inside the furnace, he strengthened the bellows supplying the blast of air. The resulting pig-iron was of good enough quality for forging into wrought iron. These advances became widely known in the 1760s and led to a rapid increase in pig-iron production.

As pig-iron became plentiful, ironmasters looked for a speedier method of refining it into bar iron. A way was found by Henry Cort, a supplier of wrought iron goods to the Royal Navy, who was based at Funtley, near Portsmouth. In 1783–4 he developed two processes which together could turn large amounts of pig-iron into good quality bar iron without the need for hammering at the forge.

The first of Cort's processes was called *puddling*. Pig-iron was placed in a special furnace which prevented direct contact between the metal and the fire (see diagram). By keeping the two apart in this way, Cort was able to use ordinary coal without spoiling the iron. When the pigs had been purified, the iron became spongy and was formed into balls or 'loops'. These were removed for *rolling* – the second of Cort's processes. The iron, still red hot, was passed to and fro between grooved rollers and shaped into rods, rails, sheets or whatever was required.

It had previously taken about twelve hours to forge a tonne of bar iron. Now the same amount could be rolled in 45 minutes. Puddling and rolling enabled the iron industry to meet the growing

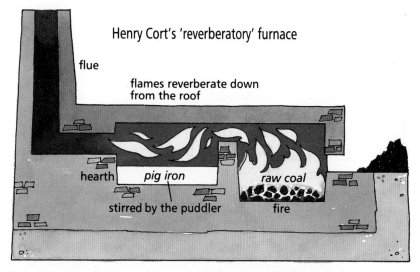

Henry Cort's 'reverberatory' furnace – so-called because the flames, on their way to the flue (outlet), reverberate (strike down) from the roof of the chamber to melt the iron.

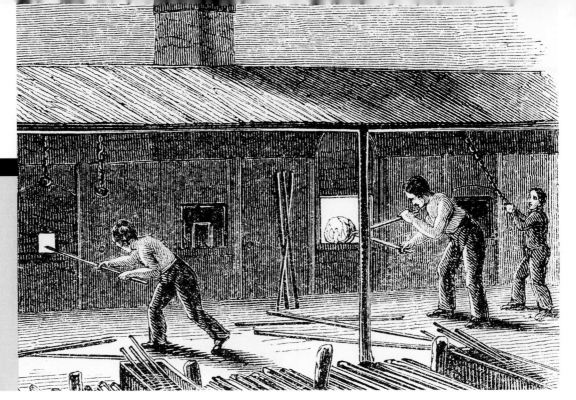

SOURCE 16

Engraving of Henry Cort's 'puddling' process. To help drive off impurities in the molten iron, a worker stirs (puddles) it with a long bar called a rabble. On the right, another man takes out a spongy 'loop' of iron with a pair of tongs.

demands being put upon it (Source 17). There was hardly an industry, from farming to shipbuilding, that did not benefit from being able to buy cheap, mass-produced bar iron.

## Changes in the coal industry

New methods of making iron and the growing use of the steam engine meant much more coal was needed. North-eastern England, around the rivers Tyne and Wear, was the chief coalmining area because of easy river and sea transport. Since the 1500s, much of its output had been shipped to London, where it was known as 'sea-coal'. Coal was also mined in other parts of the North and in the Midlands, Central Scotland and South Wales.

Coal deposits could still be found near the surface in the eighteenth century. Consequently few mine-shafts went down beyond 60 or 70 metres. As the demand for coal increased, shafts were sunk deeper. This, in turn, increased the hazards of mining, especially flooding. Chains of buckets had long been used to drain mines, but this method was slow and inefficient. Newcomen's steam-atmospheric engine made it possible to drain deep workings.

Mining was by far the most dangerous way of earning a living. Most mines contain gases capable of exploding – particularly methane, then known as 'fire-damp'. To disperse gases underground, two shafts were sunk side by side. A fire at the bottom of one shaft caused warm air to rise; this drew fresh air down the other shaft. The fresh air was directed through the mine-workings by a series of trapdoors. But this was less effective in deep mines. In the late 1700s, John Buddle, an engineer from Wallsend, near Newcastle, invented an exhaust fan to suck air out of larger pits.

SOURCE 17

The importance for the future of Cort's processes is clear from this account, written in 1862 by Samuel Smiles, an enthusiastic writer on industrial history.

After the lapse of seventy-eight years … methods of … puddling … and working the bar iron through grooved rollers – all are nearly identical with the methods of manufacture perfected by Henry Cort … The production of iron … at the time of Cort's inventions [amounted] to about 90,000 tons … Now the total quantity produced is upwards of four millions of tons … It is said that at the present time there are not fewer than 8,200 of Cort's furnaces in operation in Great Britain alone.

These original Davy safety lamps can be seen in London's Science Museum.

An Inspector of Mines, reporting in 1851, had this to say about the use of the safety lamp.

Six persons have been burnt to death by fire-damp when using the Davy lamp ... The principle of this lamp [is] not thoroughly understood by the workmen ... Davy recommended a wire gauze containing no fewer than 784 apertures (holes) in a square inch ... Lamps are now made which contain only 550 or 600 apertures per square inch ... The Davy lamp is usually adopted, but is disliked by the miner on account of the feeble illumination [it gives] ... to obtain a better light he is sometimes tempted to take off the gauze.

Miners took candles underground to light their way, but there was always the terrible risk of a naked flame exploding fire-damp. In the early 1800s, several safety lamps were invented to reduce this hazard. The best known was that of Sir Humphrey Davy **(Source 18)**. It shielded the flame with a fine metal gauze which reduced the heat given off and so greatly lessened the risk of explosion. However miners' safety lamps were often misused, sometimes with disastrous results **(Source 19)**.

More and bigger pits allowed the mining industry to keep up with the rapidly rising demand for coal. So did further technical improvements such as the use of steam engines for hauling coal to the surface. In less advanced pits women and girls were often employed to carry it in baskets up ladders. Coal output in Britain more than doubled between 1750 and 1800, from 5 to 11 million tonnes per year. It doubled again, to 22 million tonnes, by 1830. These increases were achieved by miners using only picks and shovels.

The pit-head of a Staffordshire coal-mine in the mid-nineteenth century.

I had the pleasure of viewing the Staffordshire potteries at Burslem, and the neighbouring villages, which have of late been carried on with such amazing success … It dates its great demand from Mr Wedgwood introducing, about four years ago, the cream-coloured ware … Large quantities are exported to Germany, Ireland, Holland, Russia, Spain, the East Indies, and much to America … There is no reason for fixing the manufacture in this spot, except for the convenience of plenty of coals … under all the country.

## 'The Potteries'

While textiles and iron-making were being revolutionised, great changes were occurring in some lesser industries, particularly pottery. Earthenware goods had long been made out of local clay in the villages round Stoke-on-Trent – an area known as 'The Potteries'. In the mid-1700s, this cottage industry began to be transformed, mainly through the efforts of Josiah Wedgwood (1730–95), a self-educated potter, artist and chemist.

It was discovered in the 1760s that white Cornish clay (kaolin) could be mixed with china stone to make porcelain, a much valued earthenware. There was a growing market for such goods because of the popularity of tea and coffee drinking. To meet the demand, Wedgwood expanded his business in 1769 by opening a new factory near Burslem (Source 21). He called it Etruria after the ancient Etruscans, whose vases and urns inspired many of his designs.

Wedgwood organised a *division of labour* at Etruria, similar to that of many hardware manufacturers (see Source 14). He sub-divided the skills of the potter – mixing, shaping, firing and glazing – and got each worker to concentrate on one stage of the process. Wedgwood himself supervised every detail. It is said that he broke any pot he found which was less than perfect and chalked on the worker's bench, 'This won't do for Josiah Wedgwood'.

Although Wedgwood later used steam engines for mixing clay and grinding flints, nearly all the processes in his factory were done by hand. This was true of most industries until well into the nineteenth century. Even in the 1830s and 40s, machine-minders in factories had replaced skilled hands in only a few industries. The Industrial Revolution would set the pattern for the future; in the meantime many old handicrafts continued to flourish.

Engraving of Josiah Wedgwood's Etruria factory, alongside the Grand Trunk Canal (see page 69). The canal system provided vital links to coastal ports. Barges brought in Cornish clay and carried away fragile earthenware which would otherwise have been jolted along rough roads on packhorses.

# Assessment tasks

## A Knowledge and understanding

1 'Necessity is the mother of invention.' How far is this saying true of: (a) the growth of the cotton industry from the 1760s, and (b) developments in iron-making in the eighteenth century?

2 **a** In the form of a timeline, summarise the main stages in the development of the steam engine in the eighteenth century.
   **b** At each stage, how did these developments affect British industry?

3 What do these statistics tell you about the Industrial Revolution in Britain?

Use of raw cotton in Britain

| | |
|---|---|
| 1760 | 8,000 tonnes |
| 1800 | 25,000 tonnes |
| 1830 | 100,000 tonnes |

Output of pig iron in Britain

| | |
|---|---|
| 1750 | 30,000 tonnes |
| 1805 | 250,000 tonnes |
| 1835 | 1,000,000 tonnes |

Coal production in Britain

| | |
|---|---|
| 1770 | 6,000,000 tonnes |
| 1800 | 10,000,000 tonnes |
| 1830 | 23,000,000 tonnes |

## B Interpretations and sources

4 Here two modern historians disagree about the speed of industrial change.

With James Watt's improvement ... the steam engine became the great source of mechanical energy. It was at once seen on all hands what a mighty aid to industry had arisen ... Everything now drew the industrial population towards the coalfields ... from their cottage homes ... into great towns, covering the country with continuous lines of houses, factories, mills, forges and pit-heads.
(J. Finnemore, 1955)

In most industries there was no technical revolution in the century before 1850 ... Traditional handicrafts still predominated ... [and] there had been no widespread introduction of steam-power ... Water-wheels long continued to be built and used ... The typical British worker in the mid-nineteenth century was not a factory operator ... but still a traditional craftsman or labourer or domestic servant.
(A.E. Musson, 1976/78)

   **a** On which points do these accounts disagree?
   **b** What sort of evidence would help to decide which is nearer the truth?

5 From the written sources in this chapter, list the points which help to explain: (a) the way changes in some industries encouraged the employment of children, and (b) the importance of coal in the growth and location of industry?

6 Look carefully at Source 21.

   **a** What tasks are being carried out by the steam engine?
   **b** Why would such uses of steam-power make it easier to work deep mine-shafts?
   **c** Which tasks shown here still depended upon muscle-power?

## Working and living conditions

How bad was factory life during the Industrial Revolution? Opinions were divided at the time. For example Edward Baines, a journalist and MP, thought work in textile mills was less hard than most other jobs (**Source 1**). A woman visitor to a Derbyshire mill reported that the child workers enjoyed 'reasonable hours' and slept in 'comfortable beds and airy rooms'. Yet Robert Blincoe, who had a book written about his life, claimed that as a boy he was made to work excessively long hours and had weights screwed behind his ears if he misbehaved. Masses of evidence given to parliamentary committees investigating working conditions confirmed Blincoe's picture of harshness and cruelty (**Source 2**).

### Factory discipline

Conditions varied between different industries and from one district to another. Blincoe, for example, worked in a country mill where there were few people to tell what went on. There were certainly good employers, such as Robert Owen (see page 63), who treated their workforce well. However in nearly all textile mills the hours of work were long. The usual working day was at least 12–14 hours, Monday to Saturday. This could

### SOURCE 1

Edward Baines (1800–90) published a history of the cotton industry in 1835. This was his view of child labour

It must be admitted that the hours of labour in cotton mills are long … but … none of the work in which children and young persons are engaged requires constant attention … It is scarcely possible for any employment to be lighter … The only thing which makes factory labour trying … is that they [the children] are confined for long hours and deprived of fresh air: this makes them pale … but it rarely brings on disease.

### SOURCE 2

This evidence was given by Samuel Coulson, father of two mill girls, to a parliamentary committee investigating the working conditions of factory children (1832).

*The common hours of labour were from 6 in the morning till half-past eight at night?*
Yes.
*Were the children excessively fatigued (tired) by this labour?*
Many times; we have cried often when we have given them the little victualling (food) we had to give them; we had to shake them, and they have fallen to sleep with the victuals in their mouths many a time.
*Had any of them any accident in consequence of this labour?*
Yes, my eldest daughter when she first went there; … the cog caught her forefinger nail and screwed it off below the knuckle, and she was five weeks in Leeds Infirmary.
*Were her wages paid during that time?*
As soon as the accident happened the wages were totally stopped …
*Did this excessive labour occasion much cruelty also?*
Yes, with being so very much fatigued the strap was very frequently used.

**SOURCES 3 & 4**

Two contrasting views of child labour in factories.
Right : young children winding cotton in about 1820. Left : 'Love conquered fear' - an illustration from a novel by Frances Trollope, published in 1840.

increase to 18 or 19 hours during the 'brisk' (busy) time, when trade was good.

Factory and mine workers were better paid than farm labourers. This was one reason why so many came to work in these industries. But pay could be reduced by fines for 'misbehaviour' (**Source 5**). Sometimes factory workers were paid part of their wages in 'truck' tickets which could only be exchanged at the employer's shop. Such a scheme could benefit workers if the goods were sold at cut prices, as happened at Robert Owen's mill. But many factory owners charged inflated prices.

Behind most complaints about factory life there was resentment at its discipline. The poor had always laboured long and hard on the land or in their homes. But they worked when it seemed necessary to them, perhaps to harvest a crop or complete a hand-made article for a customer. Factories, on the other hand, were organised on a strict timetable. Workers were summoned to the factory by a bell and made to mind the machines with few breaks; they had to get permission to go outside to the toilet.

In the early factories work was sometimes interrupted when the water-wheel could not operate because of ice or drought. But the steam engine, which never seemed to stop, made workers slaves to their machines. They were forced to work in silence and fined for trivial offences such as leaving an oil-can out of place. Not surprisingly, workers felt they were little more than prisoners, confined in a mill instead of a cell.

---

## QUESTIONS

1. Is there any point on which Edward Baines and Samuel Coulson (Sources 1 and 2) agree?

2. Why do you think factory owners described the orphan children who came to work for them as apprentices?

3. How might the employment of children like Mary Davis (Source 6) have been a danger to miners (see page 34)?

4. From Sources 7 and 8, can you see why mine owners employed children to work underground?

---

## SOURCE 5

Here are some of the rules from a Manchester mill in the 1840s.

The door of the lodge will be closed ten minutes after the engine starts every morning, and no weaver will afterwards be admitted till breakfast time. Any weaver who may be absent during that time shall forfeit three-pence per loom ... Weavers leaving the room without the consent of the overlooker (foreman) shall forfeit three-pence ... All shuttles, brushes, oil-cans, windows, etc., if broken, shall be paid for by the weaver ... If any hand (worker) in the mill is seen *talking* to another, *whistling* or *singing*, he will be fined sixpence.

## Working women and children

Many factory jobs, especially in spinning mills, were suited to children rather than adults. Children could climb under machinery when necessary and their nimble fingers allowed them to join broken thread easily. They were usually paid between a third and a sixth of the adult wage. As the demand for child workers grew, employers obtained orphans from parish Poor Law authorities who were glad to be rid of responsibility for them. Such children were said to be 'apprentices', but they did routine work and were not taught a proper trade. Lack of exercise, insufficient sleep and poor diet ruined their health and often deformed their bodies.

Child workers were also employed down coal mines where it had long been the custom for miners' wives and children to carry coal or look after pit ponies. In 1842 a government committee published a report about conditions in the pits. It revealed that women and girls, working underground, often carried baskets of coal weighing as much as 150 kilograms. They also pulled trucks, crawling on their hands and knees with belts around their waists and a chain between their legs. One mother told the committee, 'the belt and chain are worse when I am in the family way'. Another woman described how she had given birth in the pit and brought the baby to the surface in her skirt.

Children began work when they were four or five years old. In the mines they were employed as 'trappers' to open and shut the trapdoors controlling the flow of air underground (**Source 6**). The 1842 report was illustrated with drawings, one of which showed 'The lonely little trapper' – a child sitting alone in the darkness (**Source 8**).

The coal-owners protested that conditions were not as bad as the report

**SOURCE 6**

This comes from the report of the Children's Employment Commission (1842) which investigated child labour in the mines.

*Mary Davis*, near seven years old, keeper of an air-door in a pit in South Wales, was described … as, 'A very pretty little girl, who was fast asleep under a piece of rock near the air-door below ground. Her lamp had gone out for want of oil; and upon waking her, she said the rats or someone had run away with her bread and cheese, so she went to sleep. The oversman (foreman) … thought she was not so old, though he felt sure she had been below near 18 months.'

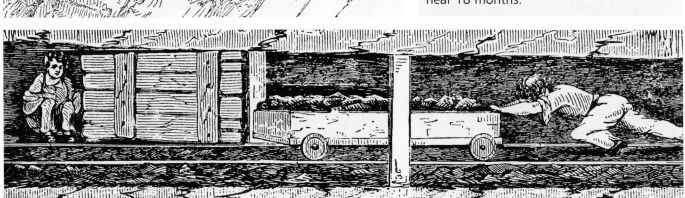

suggested. One, Lord Londonderry, claimed that trappers enjoyed their work and spent the time making clay models and drawing with chalk on the doors. MPs ignored such denials and passed a Mines Act (1842) which banned all underground work for women, girls and boys under ten. Even so, a few women continued to go down mines, often disguised as men, rather than be unemployed.

With men, women and children out working all day, there could be little family life. Some parents and children hardly saw each other except on Sundays. Mothers working long hours in factories had little time to look after their children or do household chores (**Source 9**). However it was often the wife who took charge of the family budget in the struggle to make ends meet. In many families the father was no longer the chief breadwinner and was often out of a job altogether because it was cheaper to employ women and children at lower wages.

## The industrial towns

The concentration of industry in coalfield areas changed the face of Britain. Small villages grew rapidly into manufacturing towns in many parts of the Midlands and North, South Wales and Central Scotland.

The factory woman has no time ... no opportunities of learning the common duties of domestic life ... Here is the young mother absent from her child above twelve hours daily. And who has charge of the infant in her absence? Usually some little girl or aged woman, who is hired for a trifle (small sum)...Too often the dwelling of the factory family is no home; it is sometimes a cellar, which includes no cookery, no washing, no making, no mending, no decencies of life.

In Lancashire, the population of mill towns such as Oldham and Bolton increased from a few hundred to many thousands between 1760 and 1800. During the same period Manchester, Birmingham and Glasgow became great industrial cities with populations approaching 100,000. In 1786 only one factory chimney rose above Manchester; 15 years later there were fifty.

Factory workers in the growing towns needed to be housed quickly and cheaply. Open spaces and the surrounding country areas began to fill up with poorly constructed dwellings, often built by factory owners. There were no effective building regulations and no sanitary inspectors, so houses were often damp

and proper sewers almost unheard of (**Source 11**). Rows of houses were crammed together back to back, without thought for sufficient space, light or ventilation. Between the blocks were narrow, unpaved streets, littered with rubbish and often awash with sewage. Whole families were housed in cellars, single rooms and even corners of rooms.

The new housing estates usually had little or no water supply. Water was carried from rivers, ponds or pumps. Often a single standpipe, turned on for a few minutes a day, supplied a whole street (**Source 13**). In some places drinking water was so scarce it was sold by street traders. It is therefore not surprising that infectious diseases resulting from impure water, such as typhus, typhoid and later cholera, swept through these towns (**Source 14**).

There was nothing new about dirty, overcrowded dwellings breeding disease. Such conditions had been commonplace in town and country for centuries. But the problems multiplied in the industrial towns where large numbers of people lived and worked close together. An epidemic disease which might kill dozens in a village could kill hundreds or even thousands in a town. It was this that finally forced governments to take action to improve standards of public health (see page 119).

## SOURCE 11

The evils of unplanned town development are described in this government report on Merthyr Tydvil in South Wales (1845). Merthyr was one of Britain's main iron-producing towns.

Speculators (people seeking quick profits) seem to have built courts, alleys and rows of houses wherever opportunities presented themselves, in order to meet the demand for the rapid increase of the town, entirely without regard to any order or system, and without any control as to the form of streets or arrangements for drainage … In some localities a privy (lavatory) was found common to 40 or 50 persons and more … Refuse slags from the iron works … and the river sides are frequented by persons of all ages and sexes, who manage in the best way they can.

## SOURCE 12

Factory workers' houses in Preston, Lancashire, as pictured in the report of a Royal Commission on Towns (1844). In the space down the centre, between the backyard lavatories, there was a cesspool full of sewage which was emptied twice a year!

## SOURCE 13

People getting water from a stand-pipe in Clerkenwell, London, in 1864. Here the water was only turned on for twenty minutes each day.

## The population explosion

Despite such appalling living conditions in the manufacturing towns, the total population increased rapidly during the Industrial Revolution. This provided a growing labour force and, at the same time, more and more customers to buy the rising output of goods. Britain's population went up from about 7.5 million in 1750 to 37 million in 1901 (see graph). This massive rise was made possible at first by British farmers increasing the output from the land (see page 11) and, later, by shipping in growing amounts of foreign food.

As the graph on the right shows, births greatly outnumbered deaths in the nineteenth century. There were many reasons for this. Medical discoveries and improvements in midwifery and nursing care are only part of the story. In the industrial towns people began to marry younger, which meant a wife had more child-bearing years. Moreover the demand for child workers in factories encouraged some working-class parents to have large families.

Farming improvements made available a greater variety of food, including cheese, potatoes and fresh instead of salted meat. Better methods of transport (see Chapter 7) made it easier to supply town workers with milk, dairy produce and vegetables. Plentiful supplies of coal kept homes warmer. Low priced cotton clothing – easier to wash than wool – and cheaper soap led to greater cleanliness, which in turn helped to reduce disease.

## Malthus – a gloomy forecast

The continual increase in the population alarmed thoughtful people. How would all these extra mouths be fed? A clergyman, Thomas Malthus, was sure they could not be fed unless the birth-rate slowed down. In 1798 he published *An Essay on the Principle of Population* in which he warned that the rise in population was in danger of outstripping food supplies. Malthus

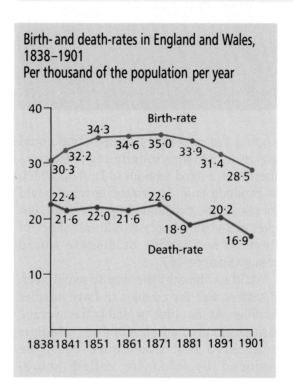

Birth- and death-rates in England and Wales, 1838–1901
Per thousand of the population per year

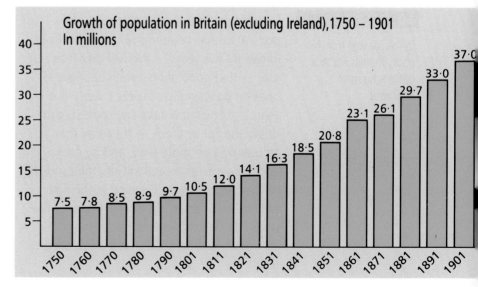

Growth of population in Britain (excluding Ireland), 1750 – 1901
In millions

SOURCE 15

The Reverend Thomas Malthus (1766-1834). He kept his name off the cover of the first-edition of his *Essay on Population* because he thought people would be shocked to find a clergyman interesting himself in such a subject!

argued that a country's population could go on increasing indefinitely, whereas there was a fixed amount of land on which to produce food. Improved farming could increase food production up to a point, but eventually the supply would fall short of demand and famine or disease would result (**Source 16**).

Malthus thought the way to avoid such disasters was for couples to have smaller families. At that time probably the average British family had six children. Malthus suggested that this figure could be reduced by what he called 'moral restraint'; men and women would have to control their sexual instincts both before and after marriage. They could also get married at an older age so as to reduce the wife's child-bearing years.

Many better-off parents used methods of birth control in the nineteenth century. Indeed, there were shops in London selling sheaths (condoms) made of linen as early as 1700. However the use of contraceptives does not seem to have become widespread among working-class couples until the early 1900s. By then, Malthus's gloomy forecast had already turned out to be wrong, for reasons he had not foreseen. Improved transport by land and sea, and inventions such as refrigeration (see page 81), allowed countries with food surpluses to sell them to places, like Britain, which needed extra food and could afford to pay for it.

In Ireland, however, Malthus's forecast proved correct. The Irish population expanded at a similar rate to that of England and Wales up to the 1840s. Then successive failures of the potato crop, on which most Irish families depended for food, left millions with hardly anything to eat. A terrible famine resulted, in which altogether $1\frac{1}{2}$ million people died (see page 80).

SOURCE 16

In this passage from his book, Thomas Malthus outlines his main argument.

In the United States of America ... the population has been found to double itself in twenty-five years ... We will take it as our rule ... that population, when unchecked, goes on doubling itself every twenty-five years ... Let us now take any spot of earth, this island for instance ... If I allow that ... by breaking up more land, and by great encouragements to agriculture, the produce of this island may be doubled in the first twenty-five years, ... in the next twenty-five years it is impossible to suppose that the produce could be quadrupled (multiplied by four).

## QUESTIONS

1. Give reasons why the birth- and death-rate both began to fall in the late 1800s? How did these changes affect the total population?

2. Was Malthus justified in basing his population theory on the USA (Source 16)? Give reasons for your answer.

3. Before the Registration Act of 1836, parish records of baptisms were kept. Why would these be less useful to historians than records of births?

4. Can you think of any reason why, according to Mr Rose (Source 18), most people did not seem to eat much fish?

## The first census, 1801

When Malthus wrote his book it was difficult to know for sure how many people lived in Britain. Parish registers of births and deaths gave useful information, but in large towns accurate records were rare. When it was suggested in 1753 that an official *census* (count) of the population should be made, the idea was rejected by MPs who were afraid it might give valuable information to Britain's enemies. By 1800, fears about the rising population made Parliament change its mind and order a census in the following year.

The *enumerators* (counters) employed to do the census were mostly clergymen and schoolmasters. They had to carry out house to house interviews because many people could not read or write (**Source 17**). The results were not always reliable. Some people were unwilling or unable to give the correct answers. For example, many said they did not know when or where they had been born.

The 1801 census was nevertheless a more accurate count of the population than had previously been attempted. Since then censuses have been taken every 10 years, except in 1941, at a time of national danger during the Second World War. To make information on population more reliable, a Births and Deaths Registration Act was passed in 1836. This made it illegal not to register births, marriages and deaths.

Censuses made it possible to calculate the rate of population growth more accurately than before. When it was found in 1811 that Britain's population had increased by 15 per cent in 10 years, concern was expressed in Parliament (**Source 18**). Census figures give many valuable clues to historical changes. In 1851, for example, the census revealed that for the first time there were more people living in towns than in the country. It also showed that over 1 million men and women worked as 'domestic servants' for the rich. By 1901 the proportion of town-dwellers had increased to three-quarters and the number of domestic servants was approaching $1\frac{1}{2}$ million!

**A census enumerator interviewing occupants of a lodging house in London in 1861. Nowadays, as most people can read and write, census forms are delivered for completion by the head of the household.**

### SOURCE 18

In January 1812, the House of Commons debated the findings of the previous year's census. The reported remarks of Mr Rose, MP, show that Malthus was not alone in fearing for the future.

Connected with the increase of population … [was the problem] of providing the people with food. Much had been stated on … the uncertainty of a supply of grain from other countries. Means should, therefore, be devised to enable the country to supply itself … by encouraging and extending the planting of potatoes, which could grow in those soils which were unfit for the cultivation of grain. There was another source of supply … the fisheries … It was strange that … fish was rare to be seen, except at the tables of the rich.

# Assessment tasks

## A Knowledge and understanding

**1 a** In what ways did the Industrial Revolution change the lives of (i) mothers, (ii) fathers, and (iii) children, of ordinary working families?

**b** Which of these changes do you think made their lives better and which made them worse?

**2** Compare the factory towns that grew up during the Industrial Revolution with what you know about (a) Roman towns, and (b) medieval towns. In each case, what were the main similarities and differences?

**3** Make a list of causes of the rapid rise in Britain's population between 1760 and 1900, and put them in what you consider to be their order of importance. Give reasons for your answer.

## B Interpretations and sources

**4** This artist's impression of 'domestic industry' appeared in a school history book published in 1955.

**a** How does it differ in detail from the historians' views which follow?

**b** Can you suggest any reasons for these differences.

Bad living conditions were not … confined to the industrial towns … There was a good deal of overcrowding in the country districts … [and] domestic workshops were usually smaller and often damper than the factory rooms.
(Arthur Redford, 1960)

Children were exploited under the domestic system, working long hours … Their parents … set them to work almost as soon as they could walk … Domestic workers … were as badly housed as factory workers.
(R.B. Jones, 1971)

**5** Look carefully at Sources 3 and 4.

**a** What impression of child labour in the early factories is each artist trying to give?

**b** Which do you think is the more accurate, and why?

**6** Compare Sources 11 and 12. How are the views they present of workers' homes similar, and how are they different?

# Religion and social improvement

## Christian reformers

John Wesley was born at Epworth, Lincolnshire, in 1703, the son of a clergyman and a deeply religious mother. On his fifth birthday his mother set him to learn his alphabet in a day. By the time he was ten he could read and write Greek. At school, he rarely played games but instead told 'instructive tales' to any pupils who would listen. When he went to Oxford University, he and his brother, Charles, formed a group for prayer and study called the Holy Club. They kept to a strict daily timetable which began at 4.00 am.

Members of the Holy Club 'tested' their Christian faith by deliberately experiencing pain and discomfort. They might go without food, or spend a winter's night lying outside on the frosty ground. One member died after such a test. The other students made fun of Wesley's group, calling them 'Bible Moths' and, because of their methodical routines, 'Methodists' – a name that was revived in later years.

### John Wesley and the Methodists

Wesley became a clergyman and went to work in the American colony of Georgia. There he met some German Protestants called Moravians whose faith seemed stronger than his own. Back in England in 1738, Wesley was attending a Moravian service in London when he experienced what he called a 'conversion'. His faith became stronger and he felt sure that Christ would save him from sin. He started to tour the country, preaching and praying.

A few parsons allowed Wesley to preach in their churches, but many refused. They

**SOURCE 1**

John Wesley (1703-91), the founder of the Methodist Movement.

**QUESTIONS**

1 Can you explain why there was a shortage of churches in the new industrial towns?

2 In Source 2, what impression of Wesley is the artist trying to give?

3 What reasons could John Wesley have had for wanting to remain part of the Church of England (Source 4 will help)?

4 Despite his intentions, why did Wesley's work lead to the formation of a separate Methodist Church?

may have been worried that his sermons would be far better than their own! Wesley was a gifted preacher who appealed to people's emotions. He could make his audiences cry with joy one minute and shiver the next as he told of the tortures awaiting sinners in hell. He also got his congregations to sing hymns, many written by his brother. Altogether Charles Wesley wrote nearly 6000 hymns, and some, such as *Hark, the Herald Angels Sing!* and *Rejoice, the Lord is King*, are still popular today.

Wesley put his main effort into preaching in the growing industrial towns. These had few churches so he held services in the open – even though this was against Church of England rules. He was not always welcome in these rough and lawless places. Mobs attacked him, throwing bricks and stones. But Wesley never gave up and many people who came to make trouble stayed to pray (**Source 3**).

During a long life, Wesley covered over 200,000 miles on horseback and preached 40,000 sermons. To make sure that those he converted did not drift away from their new-found faith, Wesley organised his followers into neighbourhood 'classes'. These were attached to local groups called 'societies' which aimed to build chapels where services could be held. Without intending it, Wesley was setting up a church within a church. Although he always thought of himself as a Church of England vicar (**Source 4**), the separate organisation he created broke away soon after his death to form the Methodist Church.

## The Church of England in the eighteenth century

Wesley's passionate preaching may have won over the poor but it was not liked by the well-to-do. Most Christians now distrusted religious enthusiasm. They could not forget the misery caused by the religious quarrels of past centuries. Since the Toleration Act of 1689, Nonconformists

**SOURCE 2**

John Wesley meets an angry crowd at Wednesbury, near Birmingham

**SOURCE 3**

In his *Journal*, on 20 October 1743, John Wesley described one of the many occasions when he was nearly killed by an angry mob.

A mob from Walsall came pouring in, like a flood, and knocked down all before them. To attempt to speak was vain; for the noise on every side was like the roaring of the sea; so they dragged me along until we came to the town ... I asked, 'Are you willing to hear me speak?' Many cried out, 'No, no! Knock his brains out' ... Others said, 'Nay, but we will hear him first' ... I broke aloud into prayer. And now the man who had just before led the mob, turned and said, 'Sir, I will spend my life for you; follow me, and not one soul here shall touch a hair of your head'.

**SOURCE 4**

John Wesley explained his attitude to the Church of England in his *Journal* for 12 April (Easter Day) 1789.

I met the society and explained to them the original design of the Methodists, viz. not to be a distinct party, but to stir up all parties, Christians or heathens, but the Church of England in particular, to which they belonged from the beginning. With this view I have ... gone on for fifty years, never varying from the doctrine of the Church at all, nor from her discipline ... Necessity was laid upon me ... to preach in the open air ... [and] to form societies.

**SOURCE 5**

These Nonconformists belonged to the Society of Friends - often called Quakers because they 'quaked' with fear of the Lord. Quakers worshipped without any order of service; they sat in silence until one of the congregation felt inspired by God to speak.

(Protestants not in the Church of England) had been allowed to worship in their own way without fear of punishment. Most preferred simple services in which ministers or members of the congregation made up their own prayers (**Source 5**). Catholics also had freedom of worship so long as they did not try to convert others.

The Church of England, commonly called the Anglican Church, was still the official state church. Its higher clergy were well paid and lived comfortable lives. The bishops in the House of Lords could be relied upon to support the government and defend the monarchy. Anglicans enjoyed many privileges. Only they could go to university and be MPs, judges, army officers or government officials.

Because of its privileged position, the Anglican Church attracted the lazy and insincere as well as the religious. Pleasure-loving students of the kind who had laughed at Wesley's Holy Club often went on to become pleasure-loving parsons! Some became rich, as it was common for members of the higher clergy to draw incomes from several parishes which they rarely, if ever, visited. In each case they paid a curate a small salary to look after the parish in their absence.

Village parsons were often younger sons of wealthy landowning families. Few had any real understanding of the poor, who were expected to be obedient and respectful to their 'betters' (**Source 6**). In particular, the Anglican Church had almost no contact with workers in the new manufacturing towns. Church leaders objected when Wesley preached to these 'forgotten' people and were suspicious that he might inspire them to riot or revolt.

## The influence of Methodism: the Evangelicals

The Anglican leaders misunderstood Wesley. Although he tried to improve conditions for the poor, he was completely opposed to any kind of violence or challenge to authority. He encouraged ordinary people to be hardworking, sober

**SOURCE 7**

Methodist chapel at Burnham Thorpe, Norfolk. By 1784, over 350 such chapels had been built, in places where there were hardly any churches.

**SOURCE 6**

This prayer written for poor people was printed in a Church of England pamphlet in about 1800.

Oh God, I believe that for just and wise reasons thou hast given mankind very different states and circumstances in life, and that all the temporal (earthly) evils which have at any time happened to me, are designed by thee for my benefit; therefore, though thou hast sought ... to deprive me of many of the conveniences of life, and to leave me in a state of poverty, yet thou hast hitherto preserved and supported me.

and careful with money, and much of his work pointed the way to peaceful reform. Wesley started Sunday schools for poor children and a dispensary in London where the needy could receive free medicine and medical advice. He was one of the first public figures to condemn the slave trade and he worked for better conditions in the prisons.

However, Wesley annoyed the Church authorities by appointing uneducated men as preachers and giving them responsible positions in his organisation. It was usual for Methodist preachers to come from the same social class as the people they served. Many early trade union leaders and social reformers learnt to speak in public in Methodist chapels. Some historians have suggested that Methodism's peaceful ways may have saved Britain from bloody revolution of the kind that occurred in France.

Not every Anglican was against Wesley's activities. Some, known as *Evangelicals* (from 'evangelist', meaning one who preaches about Christ), shared his belief that it was not enough just to pray and go to church. They too believed that Christians had a duty to live holy lives **(Source 8)** and give practical help to the poor. Robert Raikes, for example, started a Sunday school for factory children in Gloucester (1783) to keep them out of mischief on their day off and teach them

An Evangelical idea of how Christians should, or should not, behave was set out in this *Spiritual Barometer*, published in 1800.

70 Glory [in Heaven].
60 Desiring to depart to be with Christ.
50 Ardent (keen) love to the souls of men.
40 Frequent approach to the Lord's Table (communion service). Meeting for prayer.
30 Delight in the people of God; looking to Jesus.
20 Love of God's house (church) and word … Vain (undesirable) company wholly dropped.
10 Retirement for prayer and meditation.
0 Indifference; family worship only on Sunday evenings; private prayer frequently omitted.
−10 Levity (light-heartedness) in conversations; fashions, however expensive or indecent, adopted.
−20 Luxurious entertainment.
−30 The theatre … frequent parties of pleasure; home of God forsaken; much wine, spirits, etc.
−40 Love of novels … private prayer totally neglected.
−50 Parties of pleasure on the Lord's day … drunkenness; adultery.
−60 Jesting at (making fun of) religion.
−70 Death; perdition (sent to Hell).

SOURCE 9

Prisoners under sentence of death at Newgate gaol had to attend the chapel to hear 'the execution sermon' given by a priest. They were made to gather round a coffin.

## QUESTIONS

**1** Can you suggest a reason why the younger sons of landowners often became clergymen?

**2** Wesley appointed uneducated men as preachers. What were the advantages and disadvantages of this?

**3** What objections could the Evangelicals have had to reading novels and going to the theatre (Source 8)?

**4** What was the purpose of transporting criminals to the colonies rather than giving them gaol sentences in Britain?

to read the Bible. Other Evangelicals concerned themselves with prisons, factory conditions and the slave trade.

## Prison reform

Prisons in the eighteenth century were not meant to be places for long-term punishment. They were usually just temporary accommodation for suspects awaiting trial and convicts due to be executed or transported overseas to one of the colonies. However some people spent years in prison. Debtors, for example, were not supposed to be freed until they had paid their debts. This could be difficult while they were locked up and unable to earn money! If friends could not help, they tried to beg from strangers.

Prisoners were not held in separate cells. Men, women and children were herded together in filthy, overcrowded buildings. Gaolers were not paid; they lived on whatever money and goods they could get from the inmates. Wealthy prisoners could buy all the food and drink they wanted. Some were even allowed a separate room for entertaining visitors. Poor prisoners were starved, beaten and often had their clothes stolen by the gaolers.

In the 1770s John Howard, a Bedfordshire magistrate, spent a lot of his own money on carrying out a detailed investigation into prison conditions. His report, published in 1777 **(Source 10)**, provided evidence of widespread corruption and cruelty. Howard urged the government to pay gaolers proper wages

and provide sanitation, clean clothing and bedding for prisoners. He also wanted to see workshops and chapels in all gaols. However most MPs were against such 'soft' treatment of convicts. Parliament made no serious attempt to improve the prisons during Howard's lifetime.

The argument for prison reform was taken up by a Quaker, Elizabeth Fry, a wealthy banker's wife. In 1813 she visited London's Newgate Gaol, after hearing about the wretched state of the prisoners there. The experience changed her life. In one part of the gaol she found 300 ragged women crowded together, many with children, and only dirty straw for them to sleep on. When she appeared, women scrambled towards her, their eyes on the gold chain round her neck! It was a frightening moment, but her quiet manner and comforting words calmed the prisoners. Many fell down sobbing at her feet and begged for help.

Elizabeth Fry set her mind on improving conditions at Newgate. First she arranged separate lodging for the

### SOURCE 11

Elizabeth Fry (1780-1845), known as 'the Angel of the Prisons'. For over 30 years she worked tirelessly to make prisons and convict ships more humane.

### SOURCE 10

This description of Newgate Gaol in London comes from *The State of the Prisons in England and Wales,* published in 1777 by John Howard (1726–90)

In three or four rooms there were near 150 women crowded together, many young creatures with the old and hardened … On the men's side, likewise there were many boys of twelve or fourteen years of age; some almost naked. In the men's infirmary there were only seven iron bedsteads, and there being twenty sick, some of them, naked with sores, in a miserable condition, lay on the floor with only a rag.

children. Then she organised a prison school, women's sewing classes and a rota of visitors (**Source 12**). It was the beginning of a lifetime's work to make prisons more humane. She had an effect on government policy, especially in the years 1822–30 when Sir Robert Peel was Home Secretary (responsible for law and order). Prisons began to be inspected, gaolers were paid and women prisoners guarded only by women warders. Peel also got Parliament to abolish the death penalty for about half the 200 offences to which it applied, and, in the hope of preventing crime, established the first regular police force, in the Metropolitan (London) area, in 1829.

## Abolition of the slave trade

To many Christians, the greatest evil of the time was the slave trade. This had been going on since the 1500s, when European traders first went to West Africa

### SOURCE 12

In a letter dated 4 March 1817, Elizabeth Fry described a visit to Newgate to see a woman condemned to death for helping with a robbery.

I have just returned from a most melancholy (sad) visit to Newgate, where I have been at the request of Elizabeth Fricker, previous to her execution tomorrow morning ... I found her much distressed and tormented in mind; her hands cold ... However, after a serious time with her, her troubled soul became calmed ... There are also six men to be hanged, one of whom has a [pregnant] wife, also condemned, and seven young children ... He has become quite mad ... He had just bitten the turnkey (gaoler); I saw the man come out with his hand bleeding.

### SOURCE 13

John Newton was captain of a slave ship in the 1750s. He later regretted his part in this trade and joined the campaign to abolish it. Here, in his *Journal*, Newton describes the sale of some slaves in 1753.

| | |
|---|---|
| 2 June | Anchored off St Christopher (in the West Indies). Went on shore to see the agent. |
| 3 June | Agent came on board to inspect the slaves. He thought they might get a better price in Jamaica, but I told him that the men slaves were in a bad way ... they would drop (die) fast had we another passage to make. So it was decided to fix the date for their sale in three days' time. |
| 6 June | Slaves landed and all but 20 sold. |
| 8 June | One of remaining 20 slaves died. |
| 14 June | Began to load sugar for the homeward voyage. |
| 20 June | The remaining 19 slaves sold. |
| 3 July | Sent letter to my wife by a fast ship, enclosing £50 as part of [my] commission. |

to capture black slaves and sell them to the owners of plantations in America and the West Indies. The traders gave African chiefs goods such as tools, pots and pans, weapons and ornaments in return for slaves – some of them criminals or prisoners of war. In less than 300 years, 20 million men, women and children were shipped to the New World against their will.

Once on board ship, the slaves were fastened in pairs and crammed on the decks or specially built shelves. Many died of disease or ill-treatment on the long

### SOURCE 14

William Wilberforce (1759-1833). As a young man he was selfish and pleasure-seeking, but after experiencing a religious conversion he became an Evangelical Christian and devoted himself to the anti-slavery movement.

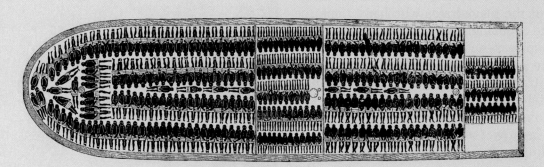

Atlantic voyage. When nearing port, the survivors were rubbed over with bees-wax and olive oil to make their skins appear healthy. Once ashore, they were sold in markets like cattle and taken off to a life of hard labour from which many soon died (**Source 13**).

The slave ships were reloaded with valuable cargoes of American cotton, tobacco and sugar for sale in Europe. Merchants and shipowners made huge profits out of this trade, so the battle to get it abolished was long and bitter. In 1785 Thomas Clarkson, an evangelical clergyman, wrote an essay attacking the slave trade. He gained many supporters, including William Wilberforce, a rich businessman and MP who was a friend of the Prime Minister, Pitt the Younger. Wilberforce and Clarkson formed a Society for the Abolition of the Slave Trade (1787) which set about collecting evidence to present to Parliament (**Source 15**).

Slave traders and plantation owners claimed that if the trade were abolished it would throw out of work sailors and shipbuilders, both vital to the defence of Britain. They also argued that if British ships stopped carrying slaves foreign vessels would continue the trade. It took until 1807 for the reformers to win a majority in Parliament. In that year it became an offence for British subjects to take part in the transport of slaves. Finally, in 1833, the ownership of slaves became illegal and all existing slaves in the British Empire – numbering at least 800,000 – were set free. A total of £20 million was paid in compensation to the slave owners.

## The Factory Acts

Within months of the abolition of slavery, in 1833, Parliament took an important step towards improving the working conditions of children in textile mills – where most of the 250,000 workers were under eighteen (see page 40). There had been earlier attempts to protect factory children but these had proved ineffective. Factory Acts in 1802 and 1819 had limited a child's

Thousands of little children ... principally female, from seven to fourteen years of age, are daily compelled to labour from six o'clock in the morning to seven in the evening, with only – Britons blush whilst you read it! – with only thirty minutes allowed for eating and recreation. Poor infants! ... Ye live in the boasted land of freedom, and ... ye are slaves, and slaves without the only comfort which the negro has. He knows that it is in his ... master's interest that he should live, be strong and healthy. Not so with you. Ye are doomed to labour from morning to night for one who cares not how soon your weak and tender frames are stretched to breaking!

NEGRO SLAVERY. | ENGLISH LIBERTY

working day to 12 hours and ordered that part-time schooling should be provided. But the magistrates who had to enforce the regulations were often friends of the employers and so turned a blind eye when the law was broken.

Caring factory owners such as John Fielden in Todmorden, Yorkshire, and Robert Owen at New Lanark, near Glasgow (see page 63) showed that shorter hours and fair treatment of workers still produced good profits. But most employers took no notice; they wanted to run their businesses in their own way. Factory owners pointed out that the jobs they offered prevented poor children from being a burden on their parents. Some claimed that their working hours could not be reduced because their profit was made 'in the last hour of the day'. For years, reformers in and out of Parliament had struggled to change such attitudes.

In 1830, *The Leeds Mercury* published a letter from Richard Oastler, a Yorkshire estate agent, which compared the treatment of factory children to that of black slaves **(Source 16)**. This marked the start of a nationwide campaign to limit working hours in the mills. The leading reformer in Parliament was Lord Ashley (Anthony Ashley Cooper, later Lord Shaftesbury), who devoted much of his life to the welfare and education of working children. His first success was the Factory Act of 1833. It barred children under nine from textile mills and fixed a maximum working week of 48 hours for the under-13s and 69 hours for 'young persons' of 13–18. Above all, the Act arranged for full-time, paid inspectors to visit factories. Employers who broke the law could be fined.

Ashley and his friends aimed to achieve a 10-hour day for all factory workers. Another Act, in 1844, went part of the way; it cut children's hours further and, for the first time, limited (to 12) the hours worked by women. In practice, this reduced men's hours too as they could not keep mills running on their own. The aim

of a 10-hour day was achieved for women and young persons in 1847 **(Source 18)**, although an extra half-hour was added in 1850.

Reformers now worked to get such laws extended beyond textiles to other trades. Women and young children had already been banned from going down mines in 1842 (see page 41). But there were many more battles to be won. One of Ashley's great campaigns was to stop the cruel practice of sending 'climbing boys' (sweeps) up chimneys to clean them. This was made illegal in 1875. The Factory Acts showed that governments were ready to take action to protect the poor and helpless, even if this meant limiting the rights of employers in their own businesses.

SOURCE 17

George Cruickshank, an artist, drew a series of cartoons attacking factory conditions. This one compares factory workers with black slaves.

SOURCE 18

Here a factory inspector describes some of the effects of the Ten Hours' Act on a family he visited in 1850.

I called in to see an old factory weaver ... [who] has three daughters ... I asked the old mother how she liked the Ten-hour Bill. She said very well; she did not know how she must do if the girls worked any longer, they ... were learning to do household work, and could sew and knit better than she could, and read very nicely too ... The old father said it was a grand thing, the Ten-hours Bill; he was learning to be a gardener and would not like to have to give it up, which he would have to do if they worked more hours.

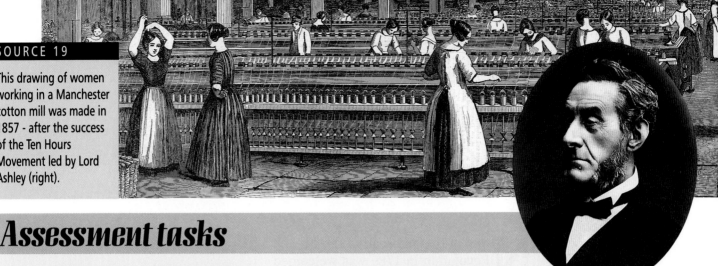

# Assessment tasks

## A Knowledge and understanding

1 In what ways did John Wesley's achievements affect religion in Britain? Try to distinguish between short- and long-term effects.

2 What ideas and attitudes had to be overcome before (a) the treatment of prisoners, and (b) working conditions in factories, could be reformed?

3 Can you suggest reasons why the anti-slavery reformers achieved their aims more quickly than the factory reformers?

## B Interpretations and sources

4 Here are three modern opinions of William Wilberforce.

Wilberforce...[and his friends] were among the first MPs to introduce into the Commons the discussion of serious issues... Wilberforce launched debates on slavery, the condition of factory workers and prisoners... He raised the tone of politics.
(Ian Bradley, 1983)

Wilberforce and the anti-slavery men introduced into English life and politics new methods of agitating and educating public opinion... He was an enthusiast who was always wise... With his talents and position he would probably have been Pitt's successor as Prime Minister if he had preferred party to mankind.
(G.M. Trevelyan, 1942)

Hero-worship makes bad history. This is particularly true of the history of the abolition movement and William Wilberforce. His friends exaggerated his virtues and achievements...Far from...[freeing] the negroes, Wilberforce actually caused them greater misery in the long run by spreading ideas of racial supremacy which justified colonialism (taking over foreign lands).
(Jack Gratus, 1973)

a What are the points of agreement and disagreement between these writers?
b Among these views, are there any that you think would not have been expressed in Wilberforce's day? Give reasons for your answer.

5 Why do you think Richard Oastler's letter (Source 16) had such a great effect at the time? Comment on (a) his ideas and (b) his use of language.

6 a What points is the artist Cruikshank trying to make in Source 17?
b How reliable is this drawing as a source of information about the lives of plantation slaves and factory workers?

# Working-class movements

News of the outbreak of the French Revolution in 1789 was welcomed in Britain. It seemed that the French were about to gain freedoms the British already took for granted. Moreover those in Britain who wanted Parliament reformed were encouraged to hear of a French government promising the people a full share in choosing their representatives. In many British towns, groups of reformers met to discuss the latest news from France and to communicate with the French revolutionaries. Because they made contact through letters they were known as 'corresponding societies'.

## Fears of revolution

As violence and disorder grew in France (see page 22), the mood of the British

(see page 22)

people changed. Those who still approved of the Revolution were regarded with suspicion. As early as 1791 a mob in Birmingham burned down the houses of local reformers. In 1792 Tom Paine, whose book, *The Rights of Man*, had inspired many corresponding societies, fled abroad to escape prosecution when his book was banned (**Source 1**). Next year, after Britain and France went to war, the government closed down the corresponding societies and arrested many of their members. In 1794 Parliament made a temporary change in the law to allow suspected trouble-makers to be kept in prison without a trial.

When the war with France finally ended, in 1815, British celebrations were short-lived. Joy turned to anger and resentment as unemployment and hardship increased. Government orders

**SOURCE 1**

Tom Paine declared that people had a right to choose their own rulers. This extract from *The Rights of Man* (1791) shows why those in authority feared him. To avoid gaol in Britain, he settled in the USA.

If I ask a man in America if he wants a king, he … asks me if I take him for an idiot. How is it that this difference happens? Are we more or less wise than others? I see in America the generality (majority) of people living in a style of plenty unknown in monarchial countries; and I see that the principle of its government, which is that of the *equal Rights of Man*, is making a rapid progress in the world.

**SOURCE 2**

King Louis XVI of France was beheaded by guillotine in January 1793. His death changed the attitude of many British people towards the French Revolution.

for armaments and military supplies stopped. This threw many people out of work just as thousands of ex-soldiers and sailors came home looking for jobs. At the same time the government abolished income tax, which had been introduced just for the war period, replacing it with taxes on goods. This hit the poor hard. Only the better-off had paid income tax, but the new taxes meant everyone, including the poorest, had to pay more for food and other essentials.

Great distress was caused by high bread prices. The war had prevented European farmers selling corn in Britain. Consequently British farmers, free from competition, had obtained record prices for their corn. The end of the war should have brought down the price of bread, as cheaper foreign corn became available. But British landowners used their power in Parliament to protect themselves against such competition. A Corn Law (1815) banned shipments of foreign corn unless the home price rose to the high figure of £4 per quarter (a measure equal to 291 litres). In the years which followed prices remained below this figure but high enough for landlords to make good profits out of expensive bread.

Discontented working people believed that things would not get better for them until they had a say in government. One who encouraged this belief was William Cobbett, a journalist whose weekly newspaper, *The Political Register*, helped to revive the reform movement (**Source 3**). Public meetings were held to call for voting rights for people other than property-owners. But the government, still fearing revolution, refused to listen to demands for reform.

In 1816, when a large reform meeting at Spa Fields in London broke up in disorder, people were again imprisoned without trial. Next year, unemployed textile workers from Manchester set off to march to London to present a petition to the Prince Regent, who was carrying out royal duties for his sick and blind father, George III. But the 'Blanketeers' – so called

because they carried blankets for bedding – found their route south barred by troops. The leaders were arrested and only one man reached London.

This print of the 'Peterloo Massacre' was made soon after it happened.

## SOURCE 6

Samuel Bamford, a weaver who became a writer, was a friend of Henry Hunt. He was arrested after Peterloo and imprisoned for a year. Here he describes the scene in St Peter's Fields.

In ten minutes ... the field was an open and almost deserted space ... The hustings (platform) remained, with a few broken flag-staves erect, and a torn and gashed banner or two dropping; whilst over the whole field were strewed caps, bonnets, hats, shawls and shoes, and other parts of male and female dress, trampled, torn and bloody ... Several mounds of human beings still remained where they had fallen, crushed down and smothered. Some of these still groaning, others with staring eyes were gasping for breath, and others would never breathe more.

## SOURCE 7

A few days after the Peterloo massacre, Lord Sidmouth, the Home Secretary, wrote this letter to the Earl of Derby.

Having laid before the Prince Regent the accounts ... from Manchester of the proceedings at that place on Monday last, I have been commanded by his royal highness to request that your lordship will express to the magistrates [his] great satisfaction [at] their prompt, decisive and efficient measures ... and likewise ... to Major Trafford his royal highness's high approbation (approval) of the support and assistance ... afforded on that occasion by himself and [those] under his command.

## 'Peterloo'

On 16 August 1819, a crowd estimated at 80,000 gathered in St Peter's Fields, Manchester, to hear a famous reformer, Henry Hunt, make a speech. The large numbers pouring into the city alarmed the authorities who called out the yeomanry – a poorly-trained, part-time force of cavalry. The crowd was already assembled and Hunt on the platform when the magistrates ordered the yeomanry to arrest him.

As the inexperienced riders pushed their way into the crowd there was mounting panic. Horses became frightened, women and children screamed. Seeing that the yeomanry were in danger of being overwhelmed, a force of regular troops, the 15th Hussars, charged the crowd. In the terrible stampede which followed, eleven people were killed and hundreds injured. The press called the tragedy 'Peterloo', in mocking memory of the battle of Waterloo where the 15th Hussars had fought four years previously (**Source 6**).

Neither the government nor the Prince Regent had any regrets about the events in Manchester. They congratulated the magistrates and soldiers (**Source 7**) and used Peterloo as an excuse to pass even stricter laws. The Six Acts (1819) severely restricted the right to hold public meetings and prevented publication of newspapers and pamphlets likely to cause unrest.

## The Reform Act, 1832

Poor people demanding the vote could be trampled on by cavalry or silenced by the Six Acts. But the government found it harder to ignore the growing number of factory-owners, merchants and other middle-class people who wanted parliamentary reform. In 1830 the Tory Party, which opposed reform, lost its majority in the House of Commons for the first time in half a century. A Whig government, headed by Lord Grey, took office and in March 1831 introduced a Bill

**SOURCE 8**

Here is part of a speech made by Lord John Russell, who introduced the Reform Bill in the House of Commons on 1 March 1831.

A stranger from afar [would be surprised] if he were taken … to a green mound, and told that this … sent two members to Parliament … or if he were shown a park with many signs of flourishing vegetable life but none of human habitation, and told that this … sent two members to Parliament. But his surprise would increase to astonishment if he were carried into the north of England, where he would see large flourishing towns, … and told that these places had no representatives in the assembly which was said to represent the people.

to reform Parliament (**Source 8**). This was passed by the Commons but twice rejected by the Tory majority in the Lords, led by the Duke of Wellington.

There were riots in many towns. Nottingham Castle was burned down, prisoners in Derby were released from gaol, and in Bristol a mob set fire to the

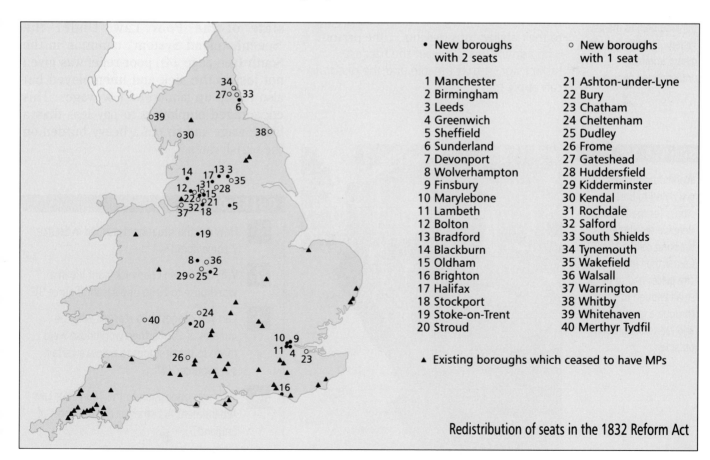

- • **New boroughs with 2 seats**
- ○ **New boroughs with 1 seat**

| | |
|---|---|
| 1 Manchester | 21 Ashton-under-Lyne |
| 2 Birmingham | 22 Bury |
| 3 Leeds | 23 Chatham |
| 4 Greenwich | 24 Cheltenham |
| 5 Sheffield | 25 Dudley |
| 6 Sunderland | 26 Frome |
| 7 Devonport | 27 Gateshead |
| 8 Wolverhampton | 28 Huddersfield |
| 9 Finsbury | 29 Kidderminster |
| 10 Marylebone | 30 Kendal |
| 11 Lambeth | 31 Rochdale |
| 12 Bolton | 32 Salford |
| 13 Bradford | 33 South Shields |
| 14 Blackburn | 34 Tynemouth |
| 15 Oldham | 35 Wakefield |
| 16 Brighton | 36 Walsall |
| 17 Halifax | 37 Warrington |
| 18 Stockport | 38 Whitby |
| 19 Stoke-on-Trent | 39 Whitehaven |
| 20 Stroud | 40 Merthyr Tydfil |

▲ **Existing boroughs which ceased to have MPs**

Redistribution of seats in the 1832 Reform Act

town hall and dozens of other buildings. In London, stones were thrown at the Duke of Wellington as he rode through the streets on June 18 – the anniversary of Waterloo. 'An odd day to choose', he remarked coldly. To prevent further unrest, the king, William IV, forced the Tory lords to let the Bill pass – by threatening otherwise to create enough new Whig lords to outvote them.

The Reform Act abolished most 'rotten' boroughs (see page 16) and distributed their seats among the counties and large towns such as Manchester, Birmingham and Leeds. It also extended voting rights. In the boroughs, owners or tenants of houses worth at least £10 a year in rent were given the vote. In the counties votes were given to better-off tenant farmers as well as the existing freeholders. Altogether, about 300,000 voters were added to the previous electorate of under half a million. Five out of every six adult males were still without the vote.

The 1832 Act gave hope of further reform. As Sir Robert Peel had said during the debates, he was against the Bill '… because I was unwilling to open a door which I saw no prospect of being able to close'. Nevertheless the actual changes made by the Act hardly justified all the fuss it had caused. The working classes realised they had got nothing from it and condemned the Act as 'the great betrayal'. All that had happened was that well-to-do landowners had agreed to share power with the industrial middle classes.

## The new Poor Law

The Whig Government was no more sympathetic to working-class opinion than the Tories had been. Its most urgent problem after 1832 was the unsatisfactory state of the Poor Law. Under the 'Speenhamland System', common in the South (see page 14), poor relief was given not just to the sick and unemployed but also to top up labourers' low wages. This encouraged employers to pay less than a living wage and so put a heavy burden on the parish rates.

### SOURCE 9

The 1834 Act followed a report on poor relief written mainly by Edwin Chadwick (see page 119). Here he explains the thinking behind the new system. By 'dissolute' he meant immoral, undisciplined people.

By "the workhouse system" is meant having all relief through the workhouse, making this workhouse an uninviting place … preventing any of its inmates from going out or receiving visitors without a written order to that effect … disallowing beer and tobacco, and finding them work according to their ability: thus making … the person who administers the relief the hardest taskmaster … that the idle and the dissolute can apply to.

### SOURCE 10

Workhouse inmates often had to break stones for roadbuilding. Here we see stone-breaking cells at Carmarthen in Wales. The pieces had to be small enough to pass through a grading grille and fall to the ground outside.

### QUESTIONS

1. How did the situation described in Source 7 come about?

2. Why did Edwin Chadwick want life in a workhouse to be so unpleasant (Source 9)?

3. Can you suggest *two* reasons why the inmates of Carmarthen workhouse were made to break stones to below a certain size (Source 10)?

4. Why was opposition to the 1834 Poor Law Amendment Act strongest in the north of England?

A Poor Law Amendment Act (1834) was designed to cut the cost of poor relief – and so bring down the rates paid by householders. In future, relief would only be given to the 'able-bodied' poor if they entered a workhouse. And to make sure that only those in genuine need applied for relief, life in a workhouse was made more unpleasant than that of the poorest family outside **(Source 9)**. Workhouses now became little better than prisons. Food was reduced to the bare minimum, work was made as hard and boring as possible **(Source 10)** and families were broken up. Husbands and wives were kept apart to stop them having children who would become a further burden on the community.

The new Poor Law was more efficient than the old and led to lower parish rates. But it was hated and feared by the poor. Opposition was greatest in the northern industrial towns. Here workers who became unemployed for short periods when trade was slack were used to receiving money relief until they found a job. The 1834 Act aimed to cut off such relief. In many northern areas the Act proved unworkable and money relief continued to be paid. But in places where the law was strictly enforced there were often mass meetings to protest against the workhouses. Grievances about this harsh law soon merged into a further campaign for reform of Parliament.

## The Chartists

In 1836 a group of skilled tradesmen formed the London Working Men's Association. Their aim was to gain for 'all classes of society ... equal political and social rights'. The Secretary of the Association, William Lovett, put its demands in a six-point charter **(Source 11)**, and so the Chartist Movement was born. Lovett believed in peaceful persuasion. His Association produced pamphlets and held public meetings to spread the word of reform.

The 'People's Charter' ... [is] the outline of an act [of Parliament] to provide for the just representation of the people of Great Britain in the Commons House of Parliament – embracing the principles of Universal Suffrage (the vote for all adult males), No Property Qualifications (men without property could be MPs), Annual Parliaments (a general election every year), Equal Representation (the areas represented by MPs to be equal), Payment of Members (MPs to receive a salary), and Vote by Ballot (secret voting).

Those who joined the Chartists in the North and in Wales belonged to the poorest section of society. Their main driving force was often hatred of the new Poor Law. They turned to a leader very different from Lovett. Feargus O'Connor was a fiery Irishman who stirred up his audiences with violent threats against the rich. His awful warnings of what would happen if the government did not accept the Charter gave hope to hungry men and women. O'Connor soon became the effective leader of the Movement.

In February 1839, O'Connor's newspaper, *The Northern Star*, printed this 'Address of the Female Political Union of Newcastle-upon-Tyne to their Fellow-countrywomen'.

We have been told that the province of woman is her home, and that … politics should be left to men; this we deny … Is it not true that the interests of our fathers, husbands and brothers ought to be ours? If they are oppressed and impoverished (poor) do we not share those evils with them? … Our husbands are over-wrought (over-worked), our houses half furnished, our families ill-fed and our children uneducated – the fear of want hangs over our heads … We are oppressed because we are poor.

In July 1839, the Chartists presented a National Petition to Parliament. They claimed it had been signed by 1,250,000 supporters, including many women. Although the Charter said nothing about votes for women, wives and daughters joined in the campaign **(Source 13)**. The Commons debated the Charter and rejected it by a large majority. O'Connor's supporters now threatened a general strike, but this fell through. Chartists from the Welsh valleys refused to give up. In November 1839, over 1000 of them, led by John Frost, a local magistrate, marched into Newport armed with old muskets and clubs. However the 'Newport Rising' was crushed by soldiers and Frost transported to Australia for life.

A second National Petition was rejected by Parliament in 1842. Riots which followed caused Lovett to leave the movement in disgust. Finally, in April 1848, the largest petition of all was paraded before a big crowd on Kennington Common in London. Talk of revolution had put the government on its guard. The aged Duke of Wellington took charge of law and order in London and ringed the Common with special constables. A planned procession across Westminster Bridge to Parliament was forbidden; instead the petition was carried in three cabs. It was found to contain many fake signatures, including Queen Victoria, Wellington and Pug Nose. The Commons rejected it by 222 votes to 17.

Chartism had become a hopeless cause. O'Connor died in an asylum in 1855. His funeral, attended by 50,000 people, was the last great Chartist gathering. Without middle-class support and with a divided leadership and confused aims, Chartism had little hope of success. There was never any prospect of the far-reaching demands in the Charter gaining majority support in the Parliament of that time. However between 1858 and 1918 five of the Six Points were accepted, wholly or partly, into the British parliamentary system.

The great Chartist demonstration on Kennington Common, 10 April 1848 - held in pouring rain. This is one of the earliest crowd photographs.

## Early trade unions

During the eighteenth century it was quite common for workers in the same trade to band together to negotiate with their employers over pay and conditions of work. Sometimes when talks broke down there were strikes. Many employers tried to stop their workers forming *combinations* – as unions were called. They were helped by Parliament which passed several Acts forbidding unions in particular trades.

After the French Revolution, the government became suspicious of all working-class organisations. As a result, Combination Acts in 1799 and 1800 outlawed trade unions in general. Many unions continued to meet secretly, however, and there were very few prosecutions. In 1824 the Combination Acts were repealed (abolished). But although trade unionists could come out into the open once again, it was still hard for them to take any action that did not fall foul of the law.

SOURCE 15

This union banner dates from the early 1820s – when trade unions were outlawed and had to meet secretly.

SOURCE 16

Robert Owen (1771-1858). Although successful in running cotton mills, his later attempts to establish 'cooperative communities' of workers, in both Britain and the USA, failed.

Small, scattered unions rarely got their way in disputes with powerful employers. It was clearly an advantage if all workers in a particular trade belonged to the same union. In 1829, John Doherty, leader of the Lancashire cotton spinners, formed a Grand General Union of Spinners. More national unions followed, in trades such as building and pottery. These were overshadowed in 1834 by the Grand National Consolidated Trades Union (GNCTU) which aimed to unite men and women of all trades.

The GNCTU was inspired by the ideas of Robert Owen, a self-made Welshman who rose from draper's apprentice to manager of a cotton mill by the age of twenty. Nine years later, in 1800, he became managing partner of New Lanark cotton mills, near Glasgow – then the largest textile factory in Britain. Owen built decent houses for his workers, cut their hours of work and provided goods at cost price in his own shops. He refused to employ children under ten, giving them free full-time schooling instead. Much to the surprise of other mill owners, Owen still made good profits.

Despite his success as an employer, Owen was against profit-making and competition in industry. In his book, *New View of Society* (1813), he suggested that workers and employers should cooperate with each other instead. The book claimed that there would be peace and plenty for all if people formed 'Villages of Cooperation'. Here they would make and exchange their products with each other on equal terms and no one would live on profits from the work of others.

Such ideas had made Owen unpopular with the ruling classes. So when he became President of the GNCTU employers were alarmed. They rightly assumed that he was interested in the union doing more than just bargaining for better pay and conditions. Owen wanted the GNCTU to bring about a complete change in the ownership and running of industry **(Source 17)**. In self-defence, employers set out to destroy the union. They ordered their workers to sign a statement, which became known as the Document, declaring that they were not members of the GNCTU. Those who refused were sacked.

## The Tolpuddle 'Martyrs'

In 1833, farm labourers in the Dorset village of Tolpuddle, faced with a pay cut, decided to join up with the GNCTU. Their leader, George Loveless, was a respectable man, although his Methodist preaching did not please local Anglicans. Blindfolded in front of a painting of a skeleton, the men took a solemn oath on the Bible. Loveless was convinced this ceremony was necessary, to impress upon each new member the seriousness of his promise.

It turned out that Loveless had made a dreadful mistake. The labourers were within their legal rights to join a trade union but the oath was unlawful – under an Act of 1797, passed to prevent secret societies being formed at a time of mutiny in the navy. The Tolpuddle landowners saw their chance to crush the local branch of the union. When the magistrate, James Frampton, heard from spies what had happened, he had Loveless and five of his companions arrested. The men stood trial at Dorchester in March 1834 **(Source 18)**. All were found guilty.

The judge could have given as little as a month in prison for the offence. Instead he imposed the maximum sentence – seven years' transportation to Australia – to make an example of the men and

---

**QUESTIONS**

**1** Why did Robert Owen's ideas make him unpopular among the rich and powerful?

**2** Why do you think the men of Tolpuddle were told to organise strike action in the way described in Source 18?

**3** How does Source 19 help to explain the severe sentence passed on the seven men of Tolpuddle?

**4** In what ways is Source 19 similar to Source 6?

---

**SOURCE 17**

This statement of aims comes from the *Rules and Regulations of the Grand National Consolidated Trades Union of Great Britain and Ireland.*

Although the design of the Union is, in the first instance, to raise the wages of the workmen, or prevent further reduction, and to diminish (lessen) the hours of labour, the great and ultimate object of it must be to … prevent the ignorant, idle and useless part of society from having undue control over the fruits of our toil … Unionists should lose no opportunity of … assisting each other in bringing about a DIFFERENT STATE OF THINGS, in which the really useful and intelligent part of society only shall have the direction of its affairs.

John Lock … We all went into Thomas Stanfield's house into a room upstairs … One of the men asked if we were ready. We said yes. One of them said, 'Then bind your eyes' … Someone then read a paper, but I don't know what the meaning of it was … It seemed to be out of some part of the Bible … We were told to kiss the book, when our eyes were unblinded … They said we were as brothers; that when we were to stop for wages (go on strike) we should not tell our masters ourselves, but that the masters would have a note or a letter sent to them.

discourage others from joining the GNCTU (**Source 19**). It had the desired effect. Before the end of the year the GNCTU had collapsed. The convicted men became known as martyrs (people who suffer for their beliefs). Despite nationwide protests, it was three years before they were pardoned and another three before the last man returned home. In the long run, however, the fate of the 'Tolpuddle Martyrs' inspired generations of working people to fight for their rights as trade unionists.

The conviction and prompt … [carrying out] of the sentences of transportation have given the greatest satisfaction to the higher classes and will, I have no doubt, have a great effect amongst the labourers, as great pains have been taken to instill in their minds that the men (of Tolpuddle) would undergo only a slight punishment, as the Union was so powerful that the Government would not venture to put the sentence into force.

# Assessment tasks

## A Knowledge and understanding

**1** What reasons could government ministers and local magistrates have had for repressing working-class organisations? Refer to the following examples of such action between 1794 and 1834:

- imprisonment of suspects without a trial
- Combination Acts against trade unions
- breaking-up of 'Blanketeers' march
- 'Peterloo', and the Six Acts
- transportation of the Tolpuddle labourers.

**2** Which sections of the population gained (a) most, and (b) least, from the 1832 Parliamentary Reform Act? Give reasons for your answers and refer to the terms of the Act.

**3 a** What were the main causes of the Chartist Movement?
**b** Explain why it failed. Refer to its aims, leadership and supporters.

## B Interpretations and sources

**4** Here are two modern views of the Tolpuddle case.

Wages rose, and in the Dorsetshire village of Tolpuddle the farmers promised that wages should be the same as in other districts. This meant a rise to 10 shillings [50p] a week. Subsequently, however, the employers deducted one shilling and then another, until wages stood at 7s. a week. Then the men were told a further reduction to 6s. was necessary. They 'consulted together what had better be done, as they knew it was impossible to live honestly on such scanty means'.
(Pauline Gregg, 1950)

In the autumn of 1830 the southern counties of England had suffered from mobs who had burned ricks and smashed up threshing machines...[The authorities] feared a nationwide conspiracy to call every worker out [on strike] at a given signal...Neither at this time nor later did either masters or men attempt to establish what 7s could actually buy... The men were not expected to pay rent; some were provided with firewood free of charge; some food was supplied in the farm kitchens, and more could be grown by spare-time labour in cottage gardens.
(S. Usherwood, 1968)

**a** List the main differences between the two accounts. Do they disagree about any of the facts of the case?
**b** What do these differences tell you about each writer's views?

**5** Re-read Sources 11 and 13.

**a** How do the general aims of the London Working Men's Association and the Female Political Union of Newcastle-upon-Tyne appear to differ?
**b** What do these differences tell you about the Chartist Movement, which both supported?

**6** Look again at Source 17.

**a** Who are being referred to as 'the ignorant, idle and useless part of society'? Why are they described in this way and, in your view, how justified is the description?
**b** What was the 'different state of things' that the Grand National Consolidated Trades Union aimed to achieve?

## Roads, canals, railways and ships

In the 1700s most roads were little more than rough tracks. They were often churned into thick mud in winter, while in summer hard ruts broke carriage-wheels and travellers raised clouds of dust. Britain's roads had been neglected since Roman times, mainly because no one wanted to pay for their upkeep **(Source 1)**. By law the people of each parish were meant to spend six days a year repairing roads. This was not a popular job. Even when it was done properly villagers worked chiefly on local roads, not those passing through the district and used by 'strangers'. Yet it was the main roads that needed improving as Britain's trade and industry expanded.

### Turnpikes and roadbuilders

A way to improve main roads was to make those who used them pay for their upkeep. During the eighteenth century groups of landowners and businessmen formed what were called turnpike trusts and got Parliament's permission to buy a stretch of road, repair it and charge for its use. Travellers paid *tolls* (charges) when they came to barriers set across the road. Most early toll-bars had pikes (spikes) on them, and this is how turnpike roads got their name.

Turnpike trusts made large profits out of the busier routes and could afford to employ engineers to lay good roads. A Scotsman, John Macadam (1756–1836), used a method still named after him. His 'Macadamised' surfaces consisted of layers of small, broken stones which were pressed and bound together by wheeled

### SOURCE 1

The writer and traveller Arthur Young (see page 13) had this to say of the road between Billericay and Tilbury in Essex (1771)

Of all the cursed roads that ever disgraced this kingdom … none ever equalled this. It is for near twelve miles so narrow that a mouse cannot pass by any carriage … The ruts are of an incredible depth … And to add to all this … I must not forget the meeting with chalk waggons, themselves frequently stuck fast, till a collection of them are in the same situation and twenty or thirty horses may be tacked to each to draw them out, one by one.

### SOURCE 2

This early-nineteenth century painting shows a coach passing a turnpike at night. The toll-keeper is on the left. Tolls were graded according to the type of traffic; the owner of a wagon, for example, would pay more than a horseman.

traffic; nowadays the stones are mixed with tar to give a waterproof 'tarmac' surface. Small jagged stones were used in a similar way, before Macadam, by John Metcalfe from Knaresborough in Yorkshire. Although totally blind from the age of six, he supervised the building of nearly 300 kilometres of turnpike roads in northern England.

Thomas Telford, a Scottish shepherd's son, achieved fame not only for his roads but also for designing and building fine bridges and canals. One of his greatest achievements was the Caledonian Canal, which formed a continuous waterway across the north of Scotland, from coast to coast. Telford's best known road, running from London to Holyhead on the Isle of Anglesey, was built to take the increased traffic between England and Ireland resulting from the Act of Union (see page 23). Its gradual slopes and bends made for faster, more comfortable coach travel (**Source 3**). To link Anglesey with the mainland, Telford built an impressive 520-metre suspension bridge across the Menai Strait.

Between 1790 and 1830 Parliament passed 2,450 Turnpike Acts for the improvement of roads. Better surfaces allowed coaches to be built for speed, with lighter bodies and thinner wheels. By the 1820s, stage coaches – changing horses frequently at coaching inns – could average 10 m.p.h. on a long run. Mail coaches, which were among the fastest, now offered a much improved postal service. With over 3000 coaches on the roads, inns did a roaring trade, feeding and accommodating travellers and stabling horses.

By the 1830s, however, the Coaching Age was coming to an end as competition from railways began to be felt. While people increasingly turned to trains, grass began to grow on many roads, coaching inns became deserted and coach-drivers and stablemen were thrown out of work. It was not until the turn of the twentieth century that the motor car began to bring life back to Britain's roads.

## 'Deadwater navigations'

In the 1750s the Duke of Bridgewater set out to develop the coal mines on his estates at Worsley, 11 kilometres from Manchester. His plan was to cut transport costs by sending his coal to Manchester on water rather than by packhorses. As

### SOURCE 3

Robert Southey, a well known poet, was a friend of Thomas Telford. In 1819 he observed Telford at work in Scotland and recorded in his *Journal* this account of his methods.

The plan upon which he proceeds in road-making is this, first to level and drain; then, like the Romans, to lay a solid pavement of stones … and a layer of stones broken to about the size of walnuts, laid over them, so that the whole are bound together; over all a little gravel if it be at hand, but this is not essential … After the foundation has been laid, the workmen are charged (ordered) to throw out every stone which is bigger than a hen's egg.

### SOURCE 4

Thomas Telford's suspension bridge over the Menai Strait, built in 1819 – 26 and still standing. The design was chosen to avoid obstruction to shipping. Tolls were charged until 1940.

there was no suitable river, the Duke had to build a 'deadwater navigation' or canal. In 1759 he put in charge of the project James Brindley, a self-taught Derbyshire engineer. Brindley had become a surveyor of great skill despite being scarcely able to read or write.

Brindley found clever solutions to some difficult engineering problems. People were amazed when he built an *aqueduct* (water bridge) to carry the canal across the river Irwell at Barton **(Source 5)**. By 1764 the Bridgewater canal was carrying coal direct from the mine-workings into Manchester. One horse could pull more on water than 60 packhorses could carry. Consequently the selling price of coal was halved and the demand for it greatly increased.

The Duke's canal was not the first in Britain. Coal was already being carried to Liverpool via the Sankey Brook navigation, built in 1757. But the Bridgewater canal became the starting point of a planned network of waterways linking the main industrial areas. Brindley's gangs of 'navvies' (so-called because they dug navigations) were soon at work on a 56-kilometre extension of the

canal, to meet the Mersey estuary at Runcorn (see map). This linked the textile towns of Lancashire with the port of Liverpool.

Brindley's most ambitious scheme was the Trent and Mersey canal, which he called the Grand Trunk. It linked the Mersey to a point on the river Trent

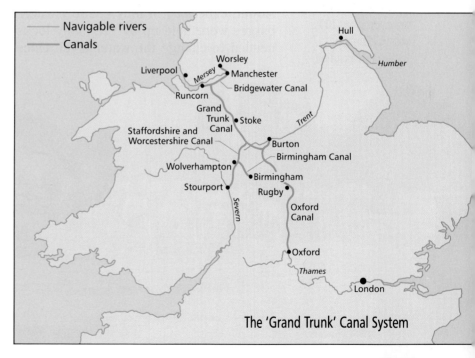

The 'Grand Trunk' Canal System

As well as carrying goods, canals were popular with some travellers, as this letter written in 1807 shows.

We left Manchester on Monday ... in a stage-boat, bound for Chester ... This was a new mode of travelling and a delightful one ... Within this floating house are two apartments ... Two horses tow it along at ... [walking pace] ... The canal is wide enough for two boats to pass ... This is the district in which ... [canals] were first tried by the Duke of Bridgewater ... His engineer, Brindley, was ... a man of real genius ... who thought of nothing but locks and levels ... and floating barges upon aqueducts.

1. How was the Barton aqueduct (Source 5) different in its purpose from ancient Roman aqueducts?

2. Why were the links with the rivers Mersey and Trent such an important part of Britain's canal network?

3. Can you suggest reasons why, even before the steam engine, mine owners laid railways rather than roads for moving coal?

4. Why were mining engineers the first to see the value of Trevithick's steam engine?

where it was navigable all the way to the Humber estuary – and so provided a continuous waterway across England, from coast to coast. Brindley planned extensions to join the Grand Trunk with the great rivers Severn and Thames, but he died, in 1772, before most of his schemes were completed.

By 1830, Britain had over 6500 kilometres of canals and navigable rivers. Although they could provide a pleasant ride for passengers (**Source 6**), their main purpose was to move heavy goods such as coal, timber, stone, clay and salt. However, as happened with road transport, the limitations of canals were exposed by the coming of railways. They were much slower, especially in hilly country where barges were held up by the many locks needed to change the water level. Once railways provided a quicker and cheaper way of carrying goods, the use of canals declined rapidly.

## Trevithick and Stephenson

Rails came long before steam locomotives. Made of wood at first, they were used in mining areas to make it easier for horses to pull wagons of coal. The first man to make a locomotive which could replace the horses was Richard Trevithick, a Cornish engineer. In February 1804 his engine drew five wagons, a coach and about 70 passengers along ten miles of railway between the Penydaren ironworks and Abercynon in South Wales.

Trevithick's invention was very different from James Watt's rotary steam engine (see page 31). It had none of the clumsy mechanism of condenser and beam because the piston was driven directly by super-heated steam at higher than atmospheric pressure. Watt had been against this because he feared the boiler would burst, but Trevithick showed that pressures several times greater than the surrounding atmosphere could safely be used.

In 1808 Trevithick took an engine to London and displayed it on a circular track

Early photograph of a horse-drawn train. Such railways were common in coal-mining areas for about 200 years before the Industrial Revolution.

near Euston Square. He called it *Catch-me-who-can* and gave rides to the public **(Source 9)**. But he failed in his aim of getting businessmen to back the invention, so he gave up and went abroad, leaving others to benefit from his work. Mining engineers in the North were impressed by Trevithick's locomotive and some built engines of their own. Among them was George Stephenson, engine-wright at Killingworth colliery near Newcastle.

Stephenson's first effort, named *Blücher* after the Prussian general (see page 24), pulled eight loaded wagons at 4 m.p.h. on its first run in July 1814. In the next seven years he built 16 more locomotives and many kilometres of track. His big chance came in 1821 when he was asked to build a rail link between the Durham coalfield and the river port of Stockton. The line ran from Witton Park colliery via Darlington, a distance of 43 kilometres. Stephenson laid the rails 4 feet $8\frac{1}{2}$ inches apart (just under 1.5 metres) – the measurement still used today. The first train, pulled by Stephenson's engine *Locomotion*, was greeted by thousands of cheering spectators in September 1825.

## The Liverpool and Manchester Railway

The Stockton-Darlington line was a financial success. It soon encouraged the businessmen of Liverpool and Manchester to build a similar rail link. In 1826 they got parliamentary permission and appointed Stephenson chief engineer. There was, however, a great deal of opposition to the project, mainly from canal companies, turnpike trusts and local landowners. The railway, they claimed, would leave a trail of ruin across the countryside, setting crops

This letter from John Hawkins, an engineer, was published in the *Mechanics Magazine* in 1847. It describes Trevithick's attempt to interest Londoners in his invention.

Observing that it is stated in your last number ... that 'the greatest speed of Trevithick's engine was five miles an hour', I think it is due to the memory of that extraordinary man to declare that in 1808 he laid down a circular railway ... [near] the Euston Road ... that he placed a locomotive engine, weighing about ten tons, on that railway – on which I rode, with my watch in hand, at the rate of twelve miles an hour; and that Mr Trevithick then gave his opinion that it would go twenty miles an hour on a straight railway.

George Stephenson (1781-1848). As a boy, his first job was minding cattle for 2 pence a day. He became an assistant colliery fireman at fourteen and ended up rich and famous.

This speech by a Member of Parliament expressed many people's fears about steam trains.

Was the House aware of the smoke and the noise, the hiss and the whirl which locomotive engines, passing at the rate of ten or twelve miles an hour, would occasion (cause)? Neither the cattle ploughing in the fields or grazing in the meadows could behold them without dismay … It would be the greatest nuisance, the most complete disturbance of quiet … that … man could invent … The beauty and comfort of country gentlemen's estates would be destroyed by it.

SOURCE 12

A modern replica of Stephenson's *Rocket*. It can be seen in the National Railway Museum, York.

SOURCE 13

In August 1830, George Stephenson gave Fanny Kemble, a famous actress, a ride on one of his locomotives. Here is what she told a friend in a letter.

You can't imagine how strange it seemed to be journeying on thus, without any visible cause of progress other than the magical machine, with its flying breath and rhythmical, unvarying pace … The engine … set off at its utmost speed, 35 miles an hour … You cannot conceive what that sensation of cutting the air was … I stood up, and with my bonnet off drank the air before me … The wind … weighed my eyelids down … this sensation of flying was quite delightful.

on fire and scaring cattle (**Source 11**). When the work started, many landowners refused to allow surveyors on to their estates or hired thugs to attack them.

The work of construction also proved difficult. Men equipped with just picks, shovels and gunpowder for blasting had to move thousands of tons of earth and rock. The greatest obstacle was Chat Moss, a huge bog which swelled in wet weather. Newly-laid track was swallowed up, drainage ditches caved in and workers had to strap boards to their feet to avoid sinking. It seemed a hopeless task but Stephenson would not give up. He had barrels laid end to end to make drainage pipes and sunk a solid foundation of earth right to the bottom.

The directors of the railway offered a prize of £500 for the best engine to work the line. There were four entries for the trials which were held in front of a large and excited crowd on a stretch of track near Rainhill. Robert Stephenson, George's son, designed *Rocket*, with a new multi-tubular boiler to give continuous steam. It won easily at an average speed of 14 m.p.h. When the Liverpool and Manchester Railway opened in 1830 all its rolling stock was pulled by Stephenson engines (**Source 13**).

## The Railway Revolution

The Liverpool-Manchester line was the world's first modern railway, with a two-way track and its own staff, stations and rolling stock. It was an instant success, carrying large quantities of goods and 1600 passengers a day. Big profits were made, which encouraged businessmen all over the country to invest in railway-building. Canal 'navvies' provided a ready-made workforce. These tough labourers toiled in all weathers and frequently risked their lives. Many fell from heights; others were killed in explosions, buried alive or drowned in flooded tunnels.

As town after town demanded a rail link, the Stephensons were in enormous demand. Between 1833 and 1837 George

was chief engineer to five projects, including the London and Birmingham line. While the Stephensons were the 'railway kings' of the North and Midlands, another gifted engineer ruled the West Country – Isambard Kingdom Brunel. He was the son of a French engineer who left France at the time of the Revolution. Isambard learnt his trade as assistant to his father who, in the 1820s, designed the first tunnel under the Thames in London.

In 1835 young Brunel was put in charge of building a line from London to Bristol. He designed every bridge, cutting, embankment and tunnel – including a 3-kilometre tunnel at Box Hill, then the longest in the world. In the years which followed, Brunel, working for the Great Western Railway (GWR), laid a network of lines across south-western England and into South Wales. Brunel laid his rails 7 feet (2.1 metres) apart – to give a faster, more stable ride. He hoped other companies would do the same, but they stuck to Stephenson's narrower gauge. The broad gauge died out after Parliament banned it outside GWR territory in 1848.

There was no attempt to plan a railway system. Parliament allowed a general 'free for all' which resulted in a haphazard network, often with more than one line running between the same towns. Nevertheless rapid progress was made. As early as 1852, nearly all the present-day main lines had been laid. By then scheduled times for fast trains between major business centres averaged above 40 m.p.h. If ever there was a 'revolution' in inland transport this was it.

Railways changed the lives of millions of people worldwide. Remote country areas were brought into contact with cities. Industries of all kinds benefited and farmers were able to sell their produce fresh over greater distances. In Britain, towns such as Swindon and Crewe grew up beside railway depots and engine repair shops. Brighton, Blackpool and other sleepy coastal villages swelled into holiday resorts as day or weekend trips to the seaside became popular. Faster travel meant people could live further from their

## SOURCE 14

This engine, capable of 60 m.p.h., was built in 1848 for the Great Western Railway's wide track by Sir Daniel Gooch, its chief locomotive designer. Notice the lack of protection for the driver and the fireman. The seat at the back of the tender was for the guard.

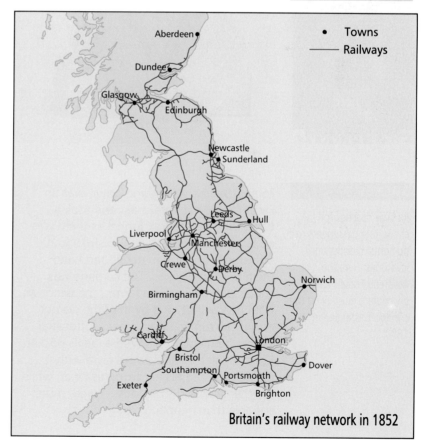

Britain's railway network in 1852

jobs, so towns spread as suburbs were built.

Britain was drawn together by railways, as journey times shrank. People of one region mingled with those of another. Newspapers and letters, aided by the introduction of the Penny Post (**Source 16**), reached their destination in hours. Every kind of organisation, from political parties to social clubs, gained from improved communications. The poor were not left out. An Act of 1844 compelled railway companies to provide at least one train a day, stopping at all stations, for 'third class' passengers. The fare could not exceed a penny ($\frac{1}{2}$p) per mile. The carriages of such trains were little more than trucks, but they had to have a roof and some kind of seating (**Source 17**).

## The coming of steamships

The earliest steam-driven boats were made before railway locomotives, as it was possible to use a low-pressure 'condensing engine' to drive a paddle-wheel. But the steamship took much longer than the steam train to establish its superiority. It was not until the second half of the nineteenth century that steamships replaced sailing vessels on the main ocean routes.

French and American engineers led the way in experimenting with steam-powered boats. The first to succeed in Britain was William Symington, a Scottish millwright. In 1802 his *Charlotte Dundas* pulled two loaded barges on the Forth-Clyde canal. Ten years later, Henry Bell's *Comet* provided a regular steamship service on the river Clyde at Glasgow. As well as her paddle-wheel, *Comet* had a sail to catch favourable winds. Larger, ocean-going

### SOURCE 16

The 'penny black' - the world's first postage stamp - introduced in 1840 as part of Rowland Hill's reform of the postal service. Stamps, by speeding up the payment of postage, made it possible to charge a standard rate for every letter, regardless of distance.

### SOURCE 15

This electric telegraph, invented in 1837 by two British scientists, Charles Wheatstone and William Cooke, was the first to be used for sending messages in advance of trains. Its five magnetic needles were made to point to letters of the alphabet by electric signals sent along wires.

### SOURCE 17

Railway coaches for cheap-fare passengers had no lights, corridors or lavatories. Here the Reverend Francis Kilvert describes a journey on the London-Bristol line in 1870.

Found the first train going down was an Excursion (cheap fare) train and took a ticket for it. In the Box Tunnel as there was no lamp the people began to strike foul brimstone (sulphur) matches and hand them to each other ... The carriage was chock full of brimstone fumes, the windows both nearly shut, and by the time we got out of the tunnel I was almost suffocated ... Then a gentleman ... seized a lady's pocket handkerchief [and] blew his nose with it ... She then seized his hat from his head, while another lady said that dogs ... were more sociable than people.

### QUESTIONS

**1** Most passenger trains had first, second and third class carriages. Why was this considered necessary? Source 17 suggests an answer.

**2** The Royal Navy preferred screw- to paddle-driven warships. Can you think of a reason why?

**3** How could a combination of steam-power and sail be an advantage on a long voyage? (Source 20 will help.)

**4** Why did it take so long for steamships to replace sailing vessels as cargo carriers?

steamships also needed sails, to save on fuel. When the American steamship *Savannah* crossed the Atlantic, in 1819, she could only carry enough coal to run the engine for an average of three hours a day.

Isambard Brunel was a pioneer of steamships as well as railways. In 1838 his *Great Western* crossed the Atlantic from Bristol in 15 days. Like all early steamships, it was driven by paddle-wheels. But these were in an exposed position and easily damaged. A better method was to drive the vessel with a propeller under the stern. The first successful ship of this kind, *Archimedes*, was designed in 1838 by an Englishman, Francis Pettit-Smith.

By this time shipbuilders were beginning to use iron instead of wood. Iron ships were stronger and cheaper to build. Brunel's *Great Britain* (1845) was made of iron and also driven by a screw-propeller. She made several trips across the Atlantic before spending 23 years on the Australian run **(Source 20)**. Brunel's most ambitious ship, the *Great Eastern*, was 215 metres long with five funnels, six masts, a double hull for safety and both screw-propeller and paddle wheels. Built at Millwall in London, she was so much bigger and heavier than previous ships that it took three months to find a way of launching her into the Thames!

The *Great Eastern* was a triumph of engineering, with room for 4000 passengers. She remained the world's biggest ship for over 40 years, yet she was never a money-making success. She burned nearly 300 tonnes of coal a day – much more than Brunel had calculated – and this made her unsuitable for the long voyage to the Far East for which she was intended. In the end her vast storage space was used for laying cables across the Atlantic to link Britain and the USA by electric telegraph. She ended her days as a floating funfair at Birkenhead.

Steamships were usually faster than sailing ships and more reliable – they did not have to wait for favourable winds. But

**SOURCE 18**

An early steamboat on the river Clyde (1813). When necessary, the tall funnel could be used as a mast to carry sails.

**SOURCE 19**

Isambard Brunel (1806-59) photographed beside the launching chains of the *Great Eastern*.

**SOURCE 20**

The *Great Britain* sailed to Australia and back 32 times. To amuse passengers during the two-month voyage, a newspaper was printed on board in 1865. Here are some extracts.

Thursday 2nd November   We were still under steam when we awoke this morning, the wind being light but favourable. At 3 p.m. the screw was taken up for a short time. The wind proving unsteady, it was put down again at 11 p.m.
Tuesday 14th   Still under steam. During last night we rounded Cape Horn; at this famous point we dreaded fearful hurricanes … Instead there is a calm which would make our noble vessel lie like a log in the water were it not for our 500 horse power machine.

Brunel's *Great Eastern* pictured in 1865 as she started to lay the Atlantic telegraph cable. Three years earlier the outer skin of her double hull had been torn open on an underwater reef outside New York harbour. She remained afloat. Any other ship would have sunk.

The *Cutty Sark*, preserved in dry dock at Greenwich, Lond Such ships were called *clippers*. With a long, narrow iron and a huge spread of sail, they were capable of high spe On the longest ocean routes, particularly to the Far East Australia, they competed with steamships as cargo carrie until the 1870s.

Engines which re-used the same steam exhaust twice, and so needed even less fuel, were fitted in ships in the 1880s. Lyon Playfair, a scientist, commented on the effects of such coal-saving in 1887.

Not long since a steamer of 3000 tons [capacity] going on a long voyage might require 2200 tons of coal, and carry only a limited cargo of 800 tons. Now, a modern steamer will make the same voyage with 800 tons of coal, and carry a freight of 2200 tons. While coal has thus been economised (saved), human labour has been lessened. In 1870 it required 47 hands on board our steamships for every 1000 tons capacity. Now only 28 are necessary.

their need to carry large amounts of coal greatly reduced their cargo space. In 1854 John Elder, a Scottish engineer, invented an engine with two cylinders which used steam exhaust from the first to drive the piston in the second. The result was a saving in fuel of nearly 60 per cent. This allowed steamships to give more space to cargo or passengers **(Source 23)**. The setting up of coaling stations on the world's main sea routes, at places such as Gibraltar, Suez and Singapore, was another vital factor in the victory of steam over sail.

# Assessment tasks

## A Knowledge and understanding

1 How did the industrial changes of the late 1700s and early 1800s (a) lead to changes in existing methods of transport, and (b) make possible new forms of transport and communications?

2 What were the consequences of railway development in Britain for each of the following:

- other forms of inland transport
- agriculture and manufacturing industry
- the growth of towns
- social life?

3 To expand the information in this chapter, look for evidence in your local area of transport developments between 1750 and 1900. Possibilities include 'coaching inns', toll-keepers' houses, canals, rivers widened to make them navigable, railways and stations (both used and disused), bridges, steamships and sailing ships on public display.

## B Interpretations and sources

4 Here are some modern views of Isambard Brunel's broad gauge railway.

When the Great Western Railway had been completed... most people preferred the broad gauge. Its carriages were roomier, they rode more steadily, the speed of the trains was effortlessly high – the Exeter expresses of 1845 were the first true express trains to run regularly anywhere in the world. These were the benefits for which... Brunel was contending.
(Jack Simmons, 1971)

Unfortunately, in the matter of the broad gauge...[although] completely successful... it came too late to prevail against a standard gauge already too securely established.
(L. T. C. Rolt, 1960)

The basic reason...for choosing a broad gauge...appears to have been speed..[However] Brunel had the body of the carriages between the wheels whereas the Stephensons had placed their carriages over the wheels so there wasn't a great [width] advantage... Brunel appears to have been blind to the problem which obviously lay ahead...In 1845 the expanding success of the GWR brought it to Gloucester where it met head on the standard gauge...Everyone – people, bags, baggage and animals – [had] to decamp from one train... to another.
(Hunter Davies, 1975)

a On what points do these accounts agree and disagree?
b What seems to be the attitude of each writer towards Brunel? Give reasons for your answer.
c What is your view? Was Brunel justified in using a broad gauge?

5 Sources 1, 6, 17 and 20 describe four journeys – by road, canal, railway and sea. Assess (a) the reliability, and (b) the usefulness, of each as historical evidence.

6 Stephenson, rather than Trevithick, has long been regarded as the father of steam railways. Can you find any clues in Sources 9 and 13 which might help to explain this?

# Trade, industry and farming in the Victorian Age

Adam Smith, a professor at Glasgow University, published a book in 1776 called *The Wealth of Nations*. It looked into the way countries traded with each other and criticised governments at home and abroad for interfering with foreign trade. Within 20 years, eight editions of the book had been printed in English and it had been translated into several languages. It was to have its greatest influence in Britain, where it became the starting point of a movement towards what is known as free trade.

## 'Free trade'

In Adam Smith's time, most of the money the government needed to run the country came from customs duties on foreign trade. Whenever it needed extra income, the government simply increased some of the duties on goods coming into or going out of the country. Adam Smith did not object to this. The thing that concerned him was that governments often used customs duties as a way of *controlling* trade. For example, the French and others could make silk goods cheaper than British manufacturers. To protect British producers against such competition, Parliament raised the price of foreign silk in Britain by putting a duty on it.

The correct principle, according to Adam Smith, was that each country should export (sell abroad) goods it could produce most cheaply and import (buy from abroad) goods more cheaply produced elsewhere **(Source 2)**. If countries stopped using customs duties to protect their home industries against foreign rivals, the overall amount of trade would increase, to everyone's advantage. Smith said the British government could get all the income it needed from import duties on '… a few sorts of goods of the most general use'. These included wine, brandy, tea and tobacco.

Such ideas appealed to British manufacturers. They were the first to experience an industrial revolution and so

### SOURCE 1

Adam Smith (1725-90) whose book started the movement towards free trade.

### SOURCE 2

In this passage from *The Wealth of Nations*, Adam Smith urges each country to concentrate on doing the things it does best.

If a foreign country can supply us with a commodity cheaper than we ourselves can make it, better buy it of them with some part of the produce of our own industry … The tailor does not attempt to make his own shoes, but buys them of the shoemaker. The shoemaker does not attempt to make his own clothes, but employs a tailor … What is prudence (common sense) in the conduct of every private family can scarce be folly in that of a great kingdom.

Smugglers secretly bringing goods ashore - to avoid paying high customs duties at the ports. To make smuggling no longer worth the risk, governments greatly reduced duties. For example in the 1780s Pitt the Younger, influenced by Adam Smith, cut the duty on tea from 119 to 12 per cent.

led the world in mass producing goods at low prices. They had little reason to fear open competition with other countries. Gradually Parliament was persuaded to abolish a wide range of customs duties. The biggest step towards free trade was taken by Sir Robert Peel's government in the years 1841–46. Peel abolished duties on over 600 articles and greatly reduced the remainder. As a result, manufacturers paid less for imported raw materials and this helped them to lower the prices of their finished goods.

By 1860, when only 48 articles continued to be taxed, Britain had become virtually a free trade country. Few other countries followed the British lead, but at the time this did not seem to matter. British manufacturers dominated world trade, despite duties put on their goods in overseas ports. For much of the long reign of Queen Victoria (1837 – 1901), it was the proud boast of the British that their country had become 'the workshop of the world'.

## The struggle over the Corn Laws

British manufacturers welcomed free trade because their goods were generally cheaper than those of other countries. Landlords and farmers, on the other hand, feared free trade because home-grown food was often dearer than that produced abroad. They claimed they would be ruined if customs duties were removed from food imports. This was the reason for the Corn Law of 1815 (see page 57). Its effect was to prevent foreign corn from entering Britain.

Keeping out cheap corn meant bread prices were often higher than they needed to be. So the Corn Law was like a tax on the majority of the people just to benefit farmers. Manufacturers and ordinary wage-earners in both town and country were against it. A new Corn Law in 1828 slightly reduced the protection offered to farmers, but it had a limited effect on bread prices. By the late 1830s a loaf weighing less than one kilogram could cost a shilling (5p) – when farm labourers earned about 10 shillings a week.

An Anti-Corn Law League was formed in Manchester in 1839. Its supporters argued that Britain's future prosperity depended upon her manufacturers; their interests should come before those of landowners. If the Corn Laws were repealed (abolished), foreigners would sell more food to Britain and, as a result, be able to afford to buy more British manufactured goods.

The League sent speakers on tours and distributed pamphlets all over Britain. Two of its leaders, Richard Cobden and John Bright, were elected to Parliament where they joined a large group of 'free

Sir Robert Peel (1788-1850). He did much to put into practice the ideas of Adam Smith. To make up government revenue lost from customs duties, Peel imposed an income tax of 3 per cent on the better-off.

This cartoon from an 1845 edition of the magazine *Punch* shows 'Papa' (Richard Cobden) taking 'Master Robert' (Peel) on a 'free trade walk'. 'That's all very well', exclaims Master Robert, 'but you know I cannot go as fast as you do'.

traders' in the Whig Party. The Conservatives (a new name for the Tories) had come to power in 1841, led by Robert Peel. Peel was in a difficult position. He had promised to abolish customs duties on manufactured goods and raw materials. This made it hard to justify treating farm products differently. But many Conservative MPs were landowners. They would consider any attempt by their leader to repeal the Corn Laws as a betrayal.

In 1845 a terrible famine in Ireland forced Peel to act. Most of the Irish potato crop was destroyed by blight: the plants withered and the growing potatoes turned black and soggy. Irish peasants lived mainly on potatoes. Other food would now have to be provided, and this meant importing foreign corn. Peel decided it was time to repeal the Corn Laws (**Source 6**). The Conservatives were split, so he needed Whig support to get his Bill through the House of Commons, in May 1846. One of the greatest political battles of the century ended in defeat for the landowners.

Free trade in corn did not stop the famine in Ireland. The potato blight got even worse and continued until 1848, by which time about one and a half million people had died of starvation and its

## SOURCE 6

This is part of a speech in the House of Commons by Robert Peel (February 1846) urging repeal of the Corn Laws. When his Bill was passed, landowners in his own party forced him to resign. It was the ruin of his political career.

The discoveries of science, the improvement of navigation … will soon bring us within ten days of New York … Iron and coal, the sinews of manufacture, give us advantages over every other rival in the great competition of industry … In skill – in energy – we are inferior to none … And is this the country to shrink from … the healthful breezes of competition? … Laws of man [should not be] restricting, in the hour of scarcity, the supply of food!

## SOURCE 7

The effects of famine in a southern Irish village are described here by a government relief worker named Caffin (February 1847). To earn money for food, the able-bodied did 'public works', usually road-building.

In the village of Scull … fever has sprung up … and swellings of limbs and body, and diarrhoea, from the want of nourishment, are everywhere … In no house that I entered was there not to be found the dead or dying … [In one] the father … was a skeleton with life, his powers of speech gone! The mother but a little better, her cries for mercy and food were heartrending … They had been well to do in the world, with a cow and a few sheep; but their crops failed, and their cattle were stolen … The son had worked on the roads … [but] from work and insufficiency of food is laid up … They had nothing to eat in the house.

## QUESTIONS

**1** How would the railways and penny post have assisted the Anti-Corn Law League?

**2** Can you explain why, in Source 5, Peel says he cannot go as fast as Cobden?

**3** In Source 6, what does Peel mean when he speaks of 'the hour of scarcity'? Why is this a reason for repealing the Corn Laws?

**4** Compare the effects of the Irish potato famine with those of the Black Death of 1348–9. What were the similarities and differences?

effects **(Source 7)**. It was a disaster to compare with the Black Death 500 years before. Many of those who survived the famine left Ireland to make their homes abroad. Most went to the USA, where two million Irish settled in the next 15 years.

## Farming and foreign competition

At first, repeal of the Corn Laws did not have the expected effect on British farming. The country was not flooded with cheap foreign corn and wheat prices remained steady for over 20 years. However, as the prices of most other goods rose in these years, doing away with the Corn Laws probably did help to keep down the cost of food.

The period up to about 1875 saw many technical advances in agriculture and steady profits for British farmers. Land drainage was improved by the use of tile pipes underground and steam power was more widely used, in ploughing, reaping and threshing. There was also a more scientific approach to farming. Research into soil chemistry led to improved manures and artificial fertilizers **(Source 8)**. Meanwhile the spread of railways enabled farmers to supply more distant markets with fresh produce.

The prosperous years ended for most British farmers in the 1870s. A series of poor harvests marked the turning point, but there were more important reasons than the weather. In countries such as the USA and Canada, railway-building had opened up vast 'prairies' for large-scale farming. And bigger, faster steamships made it possible to sell prairie corn across the Atlantic at below European prices **(Source 9)**. Most European countries quickly put up customs duties on imported food. The British government, firmly committed to free trade, took no action to protect farmers.

Owing to cheap imported corn, bread prices almost halved in Britain between 1870 and 1895. This led many farmers to turn from corn-growing to more profitable forms of agriculture. Some took up dairy

SOURCE 8

Sir John Lawes (1814 – 1900), a leading 'scientific farmer'. In 1843 he set up a research farm on his family estate at Rothamsted in Hertfordshire where he experimented with different kinds of seeds, manures and crop rotations.

farming. Others grew fruit and vegetables in market gardens near the big towns. Even so, there was no escaping foreign competition. The invention of refrigeration and canning allowed all kinds of food to be transported across the oceans. Frozen meat from Australia, New Zealand and Argentina began arriving in Britain in the 1880s. It was soon followed by butter, cheese and many other foods from the British Empire.

## Machines to make machines

The progress of science affected manufacturing even more than farming. The greatest advances came in engineering. Engineers had had nothing

SOURCE 9

R.R. Leyland, a shipowner, gave this evidence about cheap North American corn to a Royal Commission on Agriculture in 1882.

If you take first the sea transport ... the cost of working ships has diminished ... Owing to the improved style of engines ... less coal is burnt, fewer men are required to work them ... Vessels used to be ... constructed to carry a couple of thousand tons, and now it is a very common thing to have vessels employed that carry 4,000 tons ... Every line of railway ... in America, brings an additional corn-growing area into competition with the farmer here.

more than hand tools at the start of the Industrial Revolution. However by the early 1800s *machine tools* (machines which are themselves tools) were being made which could produce flat surfaces, true cylinders and accurate screw threads. An early pioneer of such developments was Henry Maudslay (1771–1831) who greatly improved the lathe – the basic machine tool. Instead of relying on the accuracy of the human hand and eye, Maudslay clamped the cutting tool to a *slide-rest*, moved by gears.

Among Maudslay's pupils were James Nasmyth and Joseph Whitworth who both set up workshops in Manchester in the 1830s. Nasmyth invented a massive steam-hammer in 1839 which could forge objects as big as the paddle-wheel shaft for a steamship **(Sources 10 and 11)**. Whitworth is best known for his classification of screw-threads (1843). On

**SOURCE 10**

A painting by the inventor, James Nasmyth, of one of his steam hammers (1871).

**SOURCE 11**

Samuel Smiles, writing in 1863, describes Nasmyth's steam hammer.

The precision and beauty of its action … were the admiration of all who saw it … It was under such complete control that while descending with its greatest momentum, it could be arrested at any point with even greater ease than any instrument used by hand. While capable of forging … the sheet-anchor for a ship … it could hammer a nail, or crack a nut without bruising the kernel.

the 'Whitworth gauge' the angle between the sides of the thread was fixed at 55 degrees and the number of threads to the inch standardised for screws of various sizes.

The achievements of British engineering were admired by the rest of the world at the Great Exhibition of 1851,

**SOURCE 12**

The Crystal Palace - home of the Great Exhibition of the Works of Industry of All Nations, held in Hyde Park, London in 1851. The iron and glass building was later re-erected at Sydenham, in South London (as pictured here), where it was accidentally destroyed by fire in 1936

in London (**Source 12**). Whitworth alone had 23 exhibits, including lathes and self-acting machines for planing, drilling, slotting and shaping. Such machine tools, along with railway locomotives, iron bridges, textiles of all kinds and an electric telegraph, gave clear evidence of the superiority of British industry (**Source 13**). 'God bless my dear country which has shown itself so great today', wrote Queen Victoria in her diary after opening the Exhibition, on 1 May.

## The age of steel

The machines on view at the Great Exhibition were made of iron. Without iron, there would have been no Industrial Revolution. Yet it was far from being an ideal material. Cast iron is brittle and liable to crack; wrought iron is too soft for many uses. Steel – iron containing a small percentage of carbon – is superior because it is both hard and flexible. But methods of making it were so slow and expensive that it could only be used for small articles such as clock springs, razor blades and cutlery.

For centuries, steel had been made by heating bar iron with charcoal to increase the amount of carbon in its surface layer. In the mid-1700s, Benjamin Huntsman, a Yorkshire clockmaker, improved the quality of this steel by heating it to a very high temperature in closed fireclay pots, or *crucibles*. But steel continued to be made only in small quantities.

In 1856 Henry Bessemer, a professional inventor, found a quick and simple method of mass producing steel. He poured molten pig-iron into a *converter*, a large vessel looking like a concrete mixer which could be tilted for filling and emptying. A blast of air was blown through holes in the base of the converter which burned out impurities and most of the carbon (**Source 15**). The resulting steel could be cast immediately into girders, rails or any other shape. Bessemer set up his own works in Sheffield in 1859 which produced steel at a tenth of the previous cost.

**SOURCE 14**

Bessemer converters in use in France. Henry Bessemer made a fortune from selling others the right to use his invention.

**QUESTIONS**

1. How would the standardisation of screw threads have helped both manufacturers and their customers?

2. Can you work out what sorts of machines are being referred to in Source 14?

3. Why was Bessemer's method of making wrought iron (Source 15) much cheaper than puddling (see page 33)?

4. Why could steel rails be made in longer sections than iron ones?

Henry Bessemer originally set out to make wrought iron in his converter. To produce steel instead, he added a little carbon and manganese. Bessemer here describes his first successful trial.

As the result of thirty minutes' blowing, wholly unaccompanied by skilled labour or the employment of fuel ... we had as much metal as could be produced by two puddlers and their two assistants, working arduously for hours with an expenditure of much fuel ... No wonder, then, that I gazed with delight on the first ... cast malleable (supple or workable) iron that the eye of man had ever rested on.

SOURCE 16

The Forth railway bridge, built of steel in the 1880s to link Edinburgh with the north of Scotland. A bridge of this size could not have been safely made of iron.

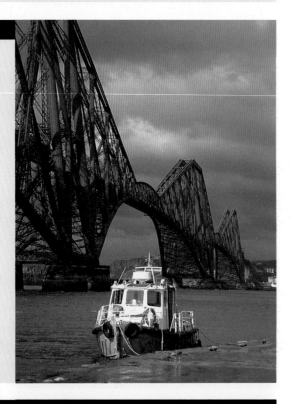

SOURCE 17

Michael Faraday (1791-1867). He demonstrated the principle of electro-magnetic induction when he showed that electric current could be generated by turning a copper disc between the poles of a magnet.

Ten years after Bessemer's discovery, William Siemens, a German living in England, found a different way of making cheap steel. He put pig-iron and scrap metal into a large shallow bath, or *open hearth*, and burned a mixture of coal-gas and air over it at a very high temperature (1650°). The resulting steel was of a very high quality. By the end of the century more steel was being produced by the open hearth process than by the converter.

Railway companies were among the first to buy large amounts of the new steel. Steel rails were made in longer sections than iron ones and could safely carry heavier locomotives. Most main railway lines had already been constructed of iron, but thousands of miles of branch lines were made of steel. Because steel is both lighter and stronger than wrought iron, it was used from the 1880s onwards in the building of big ships. And before long steel was also replacing iron in large-scale construction work (**Source 16**). Steel girders were used to reinforce concrete – a technique which led to the building of the first skyscrapers in the USA.

## New forms of power

For 100 years there was no real alternative to the steam engine for driving machines. Then, in the 1880s, two new forms of power were introduced – electricity and the petrol-driven internal combustion engine. The story of electric power goes back to 1831 when Michael Faraday first produced a continuous flow of electric current (**Source 17**). This was the starting point of both the dynamo and electric motor, although their development took years of work by scientists of many countries. Power stations were originally built to provide current for electric lighting – invented in 1878–9 by Joseph Swan in England and Thomas Edison in the USA.

The dynamos in the first power stations were driven by steam piston-engines. But they really needed an engine that could rotate faster. Charles Parsons, an engineer from Newcastle, found the answer with his steam turbine. A continuous blast of steam was forced along a tube containing a *rotor* (like a windmill, it had vanes mounted on a central shaft). This turned at great speed (**Source 18**). Parsons realised that the turbine's spinning motion was ideal for driving ships' propellers. By the beginning of the twentieth century, both warships and ocean liners were being fitted with turbines.

Meanwhile, the internal combustion engine had been developed in Germany (see diagram). It was smaller and much lighter than a steam engine, and therefore an ideal power unit for a small workshop. The new engine needed no preliminary heating-up and developed more power in relation to its weight than a steam engine. Consequently it was soon used to drive all kinds of transport vehicles.

At first, the internal combustion engine was driven by coal-gas. Before it could be used to move a vehicle, a more compact fuel had to be found that could be carried around. The answer was petrol (refined petroleum). Gottleib Daimler, a German engineer, built a petrol engine in 1883. Within four years he had used it to drive both a motor bike and a four-wheeled car. The first British motor car was built in 1896, by F.W. Lanchester. By 1903 there were nearly 20,000 cars on British roads.

## SOURCE 18

Here Charles Parsons is being questioned about the progress of his steam turbine by a Royal Commission investigating coal supplies (1903).

*Could you tell us … in what respect the turbine has advantages over the reciprocating (piston) engine?*
At the present time large turbines … are about from one-half to two-thirds the cost of ordinary engines.
*And there is … less cost of running and maintenance?*
Yes. There was a test made three weeks ago by the Cunard Company at Wallsend; the turbine at full load took 25 per cent less steam per horse-power … than the reciprocating engine.
*I understand from your evidence that the United Kingdom has taken the lead in this matter of turbines as against Germany and America?*
Yes, the United Kingdom has been first in turbines.

## SOURCE 19

A Lanchester motor car, made in 1897 in Coventry – which was from the start the main centre of the British car industry.

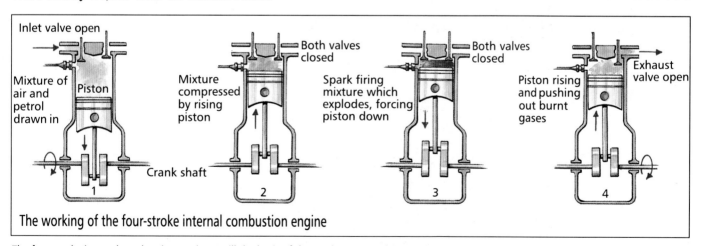

Inlet valve open

Mixture of air and petrol drawn in

Piston

1

Mixture compressed by rising piston

Both valves closed

2

Spark firing mixture which explodes, forcing piston down

Both valves closed

3

Piston rising and pushing out burnt gases

Exhaust valve open

4

Crank shaft

The working of the four-stroke internal combustion engine

The four-stroke internal combustion engine – still the basis of the modern car engine – was designed by Nikolaus Otto, a German engineer, in 1876. Although four movements of the piston are required to complete each 'firing', all the energy comes from the third stoke.

The scene was set for the car to transform people's lives in the twentieth century **(Source 20)**.

## Britain's industrial rivals

Like the farmers, British manufacturers felt the threat of foreign competition ever more strongly from the 1870s onwards. Britain's total foreign trade was greater than that of France, Germany and Italy combined in 1871. But such supremacy was about to be challenged. The USA and Germany in particular, with larger and faster growing populations, now began to take advantage of their greater resources.

After the American Civil War (1861–5), the USA's industries grew rapidly, aided by large-scale railway building. The need to supply goods to a constant stream of settlers from Europe encouraged US manufacturers to buy new machines and increase their output. At about the same time a new, united Germany, created in 1871 out of many smaller German states, was expanding its industrial production by leaps and bounds.

Britain was overtaken in steel production by the United States in 1886, and by Germany in 1893. US coal output raced ahead of Britain's in the 1890s, while Germany's was fast catching up. By then both these countries held a big lead over Britain in the making of chemicals – an increasingly important industry. More and more goods from Britain's trading rivals appeared in British shops. The government hoped to encourage people to buy British products by requiring foreign goods to be marked with the country of origin. But many people took no notice and went on buying foreign imports **(Source 22)**.

Although no longer the 'world's workshop', Britain was still the foremost trading country in 1900. Customs barriers could not stop large amounts of British goods from being sold in Europe and America. And as the Empire expanded (see Chapter 9), there was a massive increase in sales to the British colonies. British shipping dominated the world's trade routes in the late 1800s, when a third of all sea-going ships were registered in the United Kingdom. Moreover Britain had no serious rival as a shipbuilder. In 1900 British shipyards were building almost two-thirds of all the world's shipping tonnage.

---

### SOURCE 20

Lord Montagu, writing some years later, describes his experience of motoring in England in 1900.

Pneumatic tyres were in their infancy, and bursts and punctures were the rule rather than the exception. I remember also the quaint costumes we used to wear, including goggles, veils, gauntlets, and fur collars … for we had no screens in those days … The brakes on my 12 horse power Daimler car, built in 1899, were made of two pieces of wire rope to which were attached wood blocks.

### SOURCE 21

This cartoon appeared in an 1896 edition of *Punch* magazine.

### SOURCE 22

This comes from a book called *Made in Germany*, published by E.E. Williams in 1896.

You will find that the material of some of your own clothes was probably woven in Germany … The toys, and the dolls, and the fairy books … in the nursery are made in Germany … Roam the house over and the fateful mark will greet you at every turn, from the piano in your drawing-room to the mug on your kitchen dresser … Descend to your domestic depths, and you shall find your very drain-pipes German-made.

# Assessment tasks

## A Knowledge and understanding

**1 a** What were the main reasons why Britain adopted a policy of free trade in the nineteenth century?

**b** Why did Britain stick to this policy in the late-1800s despite the growing threat of foreign competition?

**2** Here are some reasons for the increasing competition from foreign farmers after 1870. In what ways are they connected?

- transport improvements by land and sea
- use of steam-powered machinery in agriculture
- Britain's policy of free trade
- opening-up of North America, Australia and New Zealand
- invention of refrigeration and food canning.

**3** How were transport and communications affected, up to 1900, by (a) the mass production of cheap steel, and (b) the invention of the internal combustion engine?

## B Interpretations and sources

**4** Here are two views of Britain's 'agricultural depression'.

Agricultural distress was general over the whole country, though there were variations in degree from county to county...Improvements were abandoned; a general rot set in...Fields chock-full of thistles became a common sight. Said the Royal Commission on Agriculture of 1882: 'All without distinction have been involved in... the distress which has fallen upon the agricultural community.'
(Pauline Gregg, 1950)

While the harsh fact of depression was undeniable for many, it was not true for all... The published statements of the time tend to reflect the views of those who had suffered most; for example, the evidence put before two Royal Commissions in 1878–82 and 1894–7 came largely from the corn counties of the south and east and does not necessarily represent the farming interest as a whole...Many people still preferred to buy the home-bred variety....of meat...Dairy farming developed considerably in the west of England; there was no danger of imported milk...The area of land put over to market gardens and small fruit doubled.
(Anthony Wood, 1982)

**a** How do these accounts differ?
**b** What are the differences based upon?
**c** Which account do you find the more convincing, and why?

**5** Re-read Sources 2 and 6. What connection, if any, can you find between Peel's speech and the ideas of Adam Smith?

**6** Look carefully at Source 21.

**a** Compare it with Source 22, also dating from 1896. Which do you think makes its point more effectively, and why?
**b** What does this source suggest about British attitudes towards Germany?
**c** What view of Britain's traders does it present?

# 9 Subjects of the Queen

## *The Empire and the Irish problem*

When this photograph of Queen Victoria was taken, in 1900, she reigned over an empire of 400 million people spread across the world. Yet when she came to the throne in 1837 the British showed no great interest in gaining territory overseas. After losing the American Colonies in 1783 (see page 21) Britain had second thoughts about the value of overseas possessions. There seemed to be little point in founding colonies if settlers were going to revolt as soon as they felt strong enough.

Why did the British change their minds and build the world's largest empire? One reason was to increase trade. Every year Britain's industries used up more raw materials and needed more customers to buy their products. Another reason was simple rivalry with other European countries trying to expand their influence abroad. A further vital factor was the growing desire, especially among poorer people, to emigrate and start a new life overseas. Despite the hardships involved **(Source 3)**, 17 million people left the United Kingdom for foreign lands in the century after 1815.

The empire gave work to farmers, engineers, doctors, soldiers, missionaries and teachers who spent their lives in the colonies. It gave power to the well-to-do, who sent their sons to rule non-Christian lands, convinced that God meant white people to do so. It gave hope to the poor, who left Britain determined to found a fairer, more equal society in a distant land.

SOURCE 1

Queen Victoria, pictured with one of her subjects from the Empire – an Indian secretary.

SOURCE 2

Emigration from Britain increased rapidly in the 1830s and 40s – a time of great hardship among the poor. In this painting by Ford Madox Brown a young couple take their last look at England.

## Canada, Australia and New Zealand

Britain was slow to realise the value of the vast, underpopulated territories of Canada, Australia and New Zealand – all acquired in the eighteenth century. The colonised part of Canada consisted mainly of two provinces: Ontario, where British settlers lived, and Quebec, populated by the earlier French colonists. Each had an elected assembly to run local affairs, but demands for greater self-government led to riots in both provinces in 1837. When order had been restored, the British sent Lord Durham, a former minister, to investigate the causes of the unrest.

The Durham Report (1839) proposed that Canadians should be allowed to manage their own affairs. Then they would have no cause to rebel, as the Americans had done **(Source 4)**. Accordingly, Ontario and Quebec were united and, in 1867, formed the basis of a *dominion* (self-governing colony). This gave Canadians control of their country yet maintained close links with Britain. Railways opened up the Canadian prairies which became vast wheatlands supplying the expanding populations of Europe.

### SOURCE 3

Poor people emigrating across the Atlantic had to put up with appalling conditions at sea, as described here by Stephen de Vere who sailed with emigrants to Canada in 1847.

Hundreds of poor people, men, women and children, of all ages from the drivelling idiot of 90 to the babe just born, [are] huddled together, without light, without air, wallowing in filth, and breathing … a damp and fetid stench … The food is … seldom sufficiently cooked … The supply of water, enough for cooking and drinking, does not allow washing. In many ships the filthy beds, teeming with all abominations, are never required to be brought on deck and aired.

### SOURCE 4

This is from Lord Durham's report on Canada. The report set out many of the terms on which Britain's later self-governing dominions were formed.

Throughout the North American Provinces there is among the British population an affection for the mother country (Britain) … which a wise and firm policy may make the foundation of a safe, honourable and enduring connexion. But … reliance on the loyalty of our countrymen may be carried too far … No large community of free and intelligent men will be contented with a position of inferiority to their neighbours (the USA) … If we wish to prevent this … it can only be done by raising up the North American colonist [to] some nationality of his own.

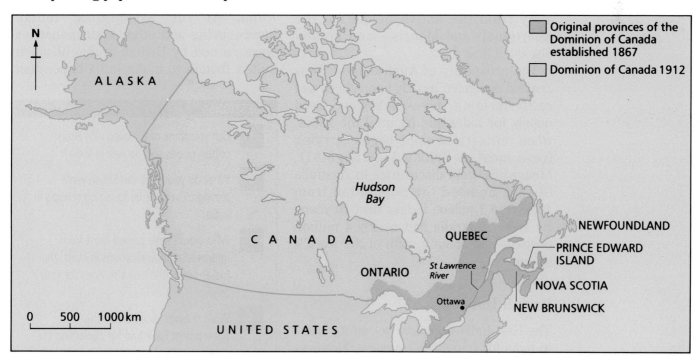

Dominion of Canada

Dominion status came later to Australia (1901) and New Zealand (1907). In Australia the majority of the population were convicts until the 1830s, when planned settlement began. Edward Gibbon Wakefield, once secretary to Lord Durham, formed a company to sell land in South Australia to wealthy settlers. He used their money to bring labourers out from Britain to farm the land. Wakefield ran a similar scheme for colonising New Zealand and went to live there himself. In both countries British settlers took land away from the native peoples – the Aboriginals and Maoris – and greatly disrupted their lives.

The prosperity of Australia and New Zealand depended heavily upon sheep and cattle farming. Livestock were bred mainly for hides and fat until the 1880s, when refrigerated ships began carrying fresh meat to Britain (see page 81). Meanwhile, gold discoveries in Australia in 1851 boosted the population from 400,000 to 1 million in less than 10 years. By 1900, Australia had nearly 4 million people – and about a sixth of the world's sheep!

## British India

The East India Company set up its bases in India for trade, not conquest. However rivalry with the French (see page 18) and distrust of native rulers led the Company to take over more and more territory to make its trading stations secure. This in turn led the British government to become increasingly involved in Indian affairs. By the early 1800s, Britain was responsible for law and order throughout India, ruling either directly or through native princes.

India provided a vast market for British goods, especially cotton textiles and hardware. By 1850, nearly a fifth of Britain's cotton exports were going to India. At the same time Indian handweaving and other craft industries were ruined by British competition. It suited Britain to make India dependent

### QUESTIONS

**1** Can you think of a reason why British cotton goods sold so well in India?

**2** What do you think the British were aiming to achieve by founding schools in India?

**3** Who would have gained most from improved communications in India, the Indians or British? Give reasons for your answer.

**4** What reasons could the British government have had for abolishing the East India Company in 1858?

SOURCE 6

British-style uniforms worn in the 1840s by *sepoys* (*Indian soldiers*) in the army of the East India Company.

SOURCE 7

Artist's impression of British troops charging Indian mutineers at Lucknow, early in 1858.

upon British manufactured goods and a supplier of food and raw materials such as rice, tea, cotton and hides. India was 'the jewel in the crown' – a source of great wealth to Britain.

The British changed India by building roads, railways and schools. They appointed thousands of civil servants to run the country and set up a cheap postal system and telegraph service. They also tried to put a stop to some Indian customs, particularly *suttee* (the burning of a wife after her husband's death). But many Indians saw such 'Europeanisation' as a threat to their religion and way of life. Lord Dalhousie, Governor-General 1848–56, caused further discontent by using troops to remove native rulers he judged to be inefficient or corrupt.

Within a year of Dalhousie's departure, a serious revolt broke out among *sepoys* (Indian troops) in the East India Company's army in Bengal. It began in May 1857 at Meerut, where *sepoys* believed a false rumour that the cartridges they had to bite open before loading in their rifles were greased with animal fat. The cow is sacred to Hindus and Muslims regard the pig as unclean. When 85 men were imprisoned for refusing to use the cartridges, three *sepoy* regiments rebelled and massacred their British officers.

Luckily for the British, the revolt did not spread over the whole country. Even so, mutineers captured Delhi, the capital, and Cawnpore, where they massacred hundreds of British men, women and children. When the British regained control, several months later, they took merciless revenge (**Source 7**). Mutineers were hanged, shot, bayoneted or blown to pieces from the mouths of cannon.

Such a narrow escape taught the British government a lesson. The East India Company was abolished in 1858 and its troops taken into the British army. The

SOURCE 8

General Neill, in Cawnpore, here describes the punishment he enforced on those held responsible for the massacre of British families.

The house in which they (the British) were butchered, and which is stained with their blood, will not be washed or cleaned by their countrymen … [but by those] who took an active part in the Mutiny … Each will be taken down to the house under a guard and will be forced into cleaning up a small portion of the blood-stains; the task will be made as revolting to his feelings as possible (by having to lick the stains) … After properly cleaning up his portion, the culprit is to be immediately hanged.

pace of change was slowed and there were no more conquests of Indian territory. New irrigation schemes helped to improve farming, although the population of over 200 million still suffered terrible famines when the rains failed. By 1900, Indians had been granted a small share in the government. But this did not quieten increasing demands for self-rule.

## South Africa – the road to war

Britain took over the Cape of Good Hope (see map) from the Dutch in 1806. It proved a valuable base for shipping on the route to India and the Far East. However the *Boers* (Dutch farmers) who had established the colony resented the arrival of the British and hated paying taxes to them. Boers used black Africans as slaves, but when Britain abolished slavery in 1833 this was no longer allowed. From 1835 onwards Boers left Cape Colony in their thousands, to get away from British rule and find more land to the north.

The Boers saw their 'Great Trek' as a journey to independence. But when the Trekkers clashed with African tribes British troops arrived to restore order. Consequently the Orange Free State and Transvaal, founded by the Boers, were never fully self-governing. This caused discontent, and in 1881 the Boers rebelled against British interference. A small British force was trapped on Majuba Hill in the Transvaal and forced to surrender. The British government hurriedly agreed to Boer demands for independence.

The British and the Boers might have lived in peace but for the discovery of gold in the Transvaal in 1886. Thousands of settlers, mostly British, arrived and a sprawling, disorderly town grew up around the diggings at Johannesburg. Paul Kruger, President of the Transvaal, saw the peaceful farming life of his people disturbed by these *Uitlanders* (outsiders). At the same time he realised that gold mining was making his country rich. He took full advantage of the situation by refusing *Uitlanders* any say in the government but taxing them heavily.

The *Uitlanders* grew discontented and some began to plot rebellion – encouraged by Kruger's bitter enemy, Cecil Rhodes, the prime minister of Cape Colony. Rhodes, an English vicar's son who had made a fortune out of diamonds and gold, dreamed of extending British rule from one end of Africa to the other (**Source 10**). He regarded the Boers as an obstacle in his path. To block their further advance, Rhodes encouraged British settlement north of Transvaal (which became Rhodesia – now Zimbabwe). He then planned to gain control of Transvaal by sending in his own British South Africa Company police to support a *Uitlander* rebellion.

### SOURCE 9

A gold-miners' compound at New Primrose mine, Johannesburg – pictured at the time of the Boer War.

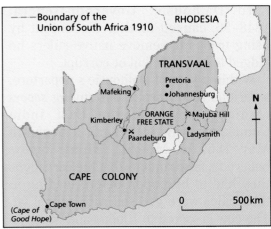

South Africa, 1815–1900

Rhodes's scheme proved disastrous. The *Uitlanders* failed to revolt, and Dr Starr Jameson, in command of the British force, grew tired of waiting. He crossed the Transvaal border in December 1895 with only 470 men and was easily overpowered. The Jameson Raid discredited Rhodes, who was forced to resign. It also convinced Kruger that the Boers would never be safe until the British were driven out of South Africa. He persuaded the Orange Free State to join him in preparations for war.

The Boer War was sparked off by a border dispute in October 1899. The Boers attacked immediately and drove the scattered British forces into Ladysmith, Kimberley and Mafeking. When the British tried to relieve the besieged towns they suffered three defeats in a week. The joyful Boers seemed on the road to victory. However, early in 1900 British reinforcements arrived under Lord Roberts and fortunes were reversed. The Boers were defeated at Paardeburg, the three besieged garrisons were relieved and by June 5 Roberts was in Pretoria, the Transvaal capital.

Many Boers refused to give in and went on raiding and ambushing the British for another eighteen months. Lord Kitchener, now in command, decided on severe measures. Ruthlessly, he sent his army to destroy farms which might shelter raiders (**Source 11**). Boer women and children were put in hastily built camps where lack of sanitation and clean water caused thousands to die from disease. Kitchener's conduct of the war was condemned by other countries, and also by many in Britain. Never again were the British people so enthusiastic about their empire.

Peace was finally signed at Vereeniging in May 1902. Transvaal and Orange Free State came under British rule and Britain paid compensation to the Boers for the loss of their homes and livestock. Five years later, however, the independence of the Boer republics was restored, and in 1910 they became part of a self-governing dominion, the Union of South Africa.

### SOURCE 10

Cecil Rhodes (1853–1902) looked beyond control of Africa to British domination of the world. He wrote this to a friend in 1891.

I contend that we (the British) are the first (best) race in the world, and that the more of the world we inhabit the better it is for the human race … The absorption of the greater portion of the world under our rule simply means the end of all wars … The bringing of the whole uncivilised world under British rule … the recovery of the United States … the making of the Anglo-Saxon race but one Empire … What a dream! but yet is is … possible.

### SOURCE 11

A British officer describes the burning of a Boer farm, on the orders of General Kitchener.

The worst moment is when you come to the house. The people thought we had called for refreshments, and one of the women went to get milk. Then we had to tell them that we had to burn the place down. I simply didn't know which way to look … I gave the inmates, three women and some children, ten minutes to clear their clothes and things out of the house … The old grandmother was very angry … Most of them were too miserable to curse. The women cried and the children stood by holding on to them, with large frightened eyes.

### SOURCE 12

Boer riflemen in trenches near Mafeking.

## 'The scramble for Africa'

Britain and other European countries had trading bases dotted along the coast of Africa. But the rest of the continent was largely unknown to Europeans until the mid-nineteenth century. Only then did explorers pick out paths into the interior and map lakes, forests, mountains and the courses of rivers. One such was David

This is part of a speech by Joseph Chamberlain, Colonial Secretary in the British government, to Birmingham businessmen in 1896.

During the last few years we have added 2,600,000 square miles to the territories … of the Queen … I can truly say that we were not the first or the most eager (to colonise) … but, if we had remained passive, what would have happened? The greater part of Africa would have been occupied by our commercial rivals who would have closed this great potential market to British trade … We, in our colonial policy, as fast as we acquire new territory … develop it for the commerce of the world.

SOURCE 13

The Victoria Falls, in modern Zimbabwe – discovered in the 1850s by the explorer David Livingstone.

Livingstone, a Scotsman, who risked death from disease and hostile tribes to become the first white man to set eyes on great landmarks like the Victoria Falls and Lake Nyasa.

African exploration revealed new sources of wealth, including mineral ores, vegetable oils and timber such as teak and mahogany. Between about 1870 and 1900, Britain and other European states competed to share out the continent in what became known as 'the Scramble for Africa' **(Source 14)**. Spear-throwing tribesmen were powerless to resist the white man's warships and guns. Even more than the search for trade, the 'Scramble' arose from rivalries between the nations of Europe. Colonies were seen as a way of increasing a country's power and influence in the world.

In 1875 a tenth of Africa was ruled by Europeans; by 1900 more than nine-tenths had been colonised (see map). France, Belgium, Portugal, Germany and Italy all claimed a share, but Britain led the way in colonising the more fertile regions, including the Gold Coast (now Ghana), Nigeria and large parts of East Africa. The Europeans ignored the customs of those they conquered and imposed their own ways, including the Christian religion. As it turned out, Britain's trade with Africa was worth much less than that with the more developed parts of the empire.

The African scramble brought Britain and France close to war in 1898. The crisis arose in the Sudan, where there was

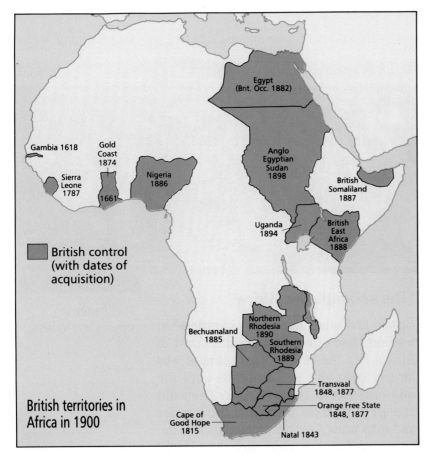

Gambia 1618

Gold Coast 1874

Sierra Leone 1787

1661

Nigeria 1886

Egypt (Brit. Occ. 1882)

Anglo Egyptian Sudan 1898

British Somaliland 1887

Uganda 1894

British East Africa 1888

British control (with dates of acquisition)

Northern Rhodesia 1890

Bechuanaland 1885

Southern Rhodesia 1889

Transvaal 1848, 1877

Orange Free State 1848, 1877

British territories in Africa in 1900

Cape of Good Hope 1815

Natal 1843

SOURCE 15

In February 1867, Fenians planned a daring raid on a store of armaments at Chester Castle in England. This report comes from *The Illustrated Times*.

The Fenians ... resolved to attack Chester Castle ... seize the arms deposited there, cut the telegraph wires, tear up the rails, and make good their escape ... [However] an ex-officer of the Fenian service had revealed the whole plot ... Prompt measures were taken ... Over 500 citizens were sworn in as special constables and paraded through the town ... During the night the Fenians evidently came to the conclusion that the preparations were too much for them ... Parties of tens and twenties were seen leaving on foot for Warrington and other neighbouring towns.

competition to control the upper waters of the Nile. British troops under Kitchener were in command of the Sudan when they came across a French flag flying over a fort on the Nile, at Fashoda. It was the work of Captain Marchand of the French army who had been sent by his government with a small force to claim the area. The British Government, knowing its military position was stronger, alerted its forces while crowds in the streets shouted for war. Reluctantly, the French gave way and ordered Marchand to leave.

## Troubles in Ireland

Ireland never recovered from the famine of the 1840s (see page 80). The emigration it caused, mainly to the USA, almost halved the population in the next 50 years. The Irish blamed Britain for the tragedy. They knew that while people were dying of starvation corn crops from British-owned estates in Ireland were being sold abroad. Meanwhile foreign grain sent by the British government proved insufficient. In 1857 resentful Irishmen in the USA founded the Fenian Society which aimed to achieve an Irish republic

independent of Britain. Fenians organised violent demonstrations in Ireland and England to publicise their cause (**Source 15**).

In 1868 William Gladstone, Britain's prime minister, decided to 'pacify Ireland' by removing some Irish grievances. To please the Catholic majority, he cut all government links with the Irish Protestant Church, taking away its property and giving much of its money to charity. Gladstone then turned to a more urgent problem. Large areas of Ireland were owned by landlords living in England who were only interested in the profits they got from their property. Peasants were often *evicted* (thrown out) of their cottages just to make way for tenants who could pay more rent. Gladstone's Land Act (1870) ordered landlords to compensate evicted tenants for any improvements they had made.

SOURCE 16

Artist's impression of poor Irish peasants being evicted from their rented cottage.

SOURCE 17

The treatment Captain Boycott describes in this letter to the *Times* in 1880 was the work of the Land League, an organisation which fought against the eviction of peasants. The League later denied Boycott's charges of theft and damage.

The people collected in crowds upon my farm, and some hundred or so came up to my house and ordered off, under threats ... all my farm labourers ... My blacksmith has received a letter threatening him with murder if he does any more work for me ... The shopkeepers have been warned to stop all supplies to my house ... My crops are trampled upon, carried away in quantities and destroyed ... my [live]stock driven out on the road ... My ruin is the object of the Land League.

This reform did not stop evictions. Nor did it stop homeless peasants taking revenge by injuring cattle, burning hay ricks and houses, and even murdering landlords. When a land agent named Boycott evicted a family, nobody would work for him or supply him with goods (**Source 17**). Many landlords were 'boycotted' in this way, which gave a new word to the English language.

## The struggle over Home Rule

Gladstone decided that his reforms needed to go further. A second Land Act (1881) stated that tenants could not be evicted so long as they paid their rent. It also set up land courts to fix fair rents in cases where landlord and tenant disagreed. Even so, this was not enough to satisfy the Irish party in the House of Commons. It demanded nothing less than 'Home Rule' by a separate Irish parliament. Meanwhile violence against landlords continued.

In 1886, Gladstone finally accepted the Irish demand to be self-governing and introduced a Home Rule Bill. It was supported by Irish MPs but defeated by an alliance of Conservatives and some of his own supporters in the Liberal party. The main stumbling block was the Protestant population in the northern countries of Ireland (known as Ulster). They preferred to remain part of the United Kingdom rather than be outnumbered by Catholics in an Irish parliament (**Source 19**). Most of Ireland's industries were in Ulster and its people were generally better-off. They had no wish to pay higher taxes to support the poorer South.

Gladstone tried again to achieve Irish Home Rule in 1893. His Bill passed the House of Commons but was defeated overwhelmingly in the Lords. At that time the Commons had no power to force its will on the Lords when the two Houses disagreed. The longer the argument about Ireland's future went on, the more determined the people of Ulster became to resist Irish independence – by force if necessary. At the same time, opposition in southern Ireland to any form of British rule hardened. The result was the *partition* (division) of Ireland in 1921. Southern Ireland became independent while Ulster remained part of the United Kingdom.

### SOURCE 18

William Ewart Gladstone (1809 – 98). A Liberal, he was prime minister on four separate occasions between 1868 and 1894, when he retired from office at the age of 84.

### SOURCE 19

Speaking in favour of the Home Rule Bill, on 7 June 1886, Gladstone told the House of Commons that Ulster could not be made an exception.

The voice of Ireland, as a whole, is at this moment clearly spoken … Five-sixths of its lawfully chosen representatives (MPs) are of one mind … I cannot allow it to be said that a Protestant minority in Ulster, or elsewhere, is to rule the question at large for Ireland … But I think that the Protestant minority should have its wishes considered to the utmost practicable extent … One scheme is that … a portion of Ulster should be excluded from the operation of the Bill … But [no scheme of this kind] has appeared to us to be so completely justified … as to warrant our including it in the Bill.

### QUESTIONS

1. What were 'five-sixths' of Irish MPs agreed about (Source 19)?

2. What did the remaining one-sixth want, and why?

3. Why did people in Ulster assume that, under Home Rule, they would have to pay higher taxes than those in the South?

4. Can you think of any reason why opposition to Irish Home Rule was stronger in the House of Lords than in the Commons?

# Assessment tasks

## A Knowledge and understanding

1 In what ways do you think life got better for the Indian people under British rule, and how did it change for the worse? Give reasons for your answer.

2 Here are five possible causes of the Boer War, 1899–1902. You may be able to add more.

- The Boers underestimated British power, after their victory at Majuba Hill.
- Cecil Rhodes's plans to extend British rule in Africa.
- The different attitudes of the Boers and British to black Africans.
- The Jameson Raid, 1895.
- President Kruger's treatment of the goldminers (*Uitlanders*).

Place these in what you consider to be their order of importance. Give reasons for your answer.

3 a What were the main grievances of Irish people against the British?
b Why did Gladstone fail (i) to 'pacify' Ireland, and (ii) to give Ireland self-government?

## B Interpretations and sources

4 Britain's Indian empire became independent, and was divided into the self-governing states of India and Pakistan, on 15 August 1947. That morning, the *Times* commented as follows.

The co-operation and compromise ... [shown by] Indian leaders ... are British qualities, and the political ideas and methods for ... [achieving] liberty with order ... are Britain's special gift to mankind. That Indian minds are now enriched by them is the result of the ... work, maintained for generations, of British men and women who under the Indian sun and at the sacrifice of domestic happiness did their duty ... before God and man.

Jawaharlal Nehru, soon to become India's leader (1948–64), had a different view of British rule.

India had to bear the cost of her own conquest ... Government was also run on a lavish and extravagant scale, all the highly paid positions being reserved for Europeans ... Nearly all our major problems today have grown up during British rule and as a direct result of British policy: ... the lack of industry and the neglect of agriculture; the extreme backwardness in the social services; and, above all, the tragic poverty of the people.

a What different views of British rule do these accounts give?
b Are these differences based on historical evidence, the opinions of the writers, or both? Give reasons for your answer.

5 a What do Sources 2 and 3 tell us about the hardships experienced by many emigrants?
b What do you think are the advantages and disadvantages of these two types of source?

6 What do Sources 4, 7, 10, 11 and 14 reveal about the strengths and weaknesses of Britain's policy towards her empire?

# The rise of the working classes

Samuel Smiles, a Scottish doctor, wrote books about inventors and engineers who rose from poor beginnings to achieve wealth and fame. He believed that the key to their success was hard work; there was no other way out of poverty. In a book called *Self-Help* (1859), Smiles had this advice for the poor: 'spend less than you earn ... scrape and save, and the pile of gold will gradually rise.'

Such ideas appealed to better-off people living comfortable lives. But in practice it took ability, ambition and often a lot of luck for people from poor families to improve their position in the world. Self-help was wishful thinking so far as most unskilled labourers were concerned. They could rarely make ends meet while in regular work, let alone when they were unemployed, injured or sick. In Victorian times there were no state schemes of social security for those who suffered hardship; just the dreaded workhouse as a last resort for the destitute.

## Friendly societies and co-operatives

Skilled, better-paid workers could, and did, help themselves. They could afford to join friendly societies. These were working men's clubs which collected weekly subscriptions from members and paid out cash benefits in times of need. Such societies had existed in one form or another at least since the seventeenth century. In 1801 there were about 7000 of them in Britain. Most were small, local organisations, but by the mid-1800s a few, such as the Oddfellows and Foresters, had branches all over the country.

Workers who could not afford to join a friendly society often belonged to a co-operative. Many of these were just grocery shops which bought goods in bulk and sold to members at reduced prices. However some co-operatives, influenced by the ideas of Robert Owen (see page 63), tried to produce goods on a non-profit making basis. There were 500 co-operatives in Britain by the early 1830s, but most lacked the necessary funds to finance their schemes and were short-lived.

The modern co-operative movement grew out of a grocery store in Toad Lane, Rochdale, set up in 1844 by a group of flannel-weavers who called themselves the Rochdale Society of Equitable Pioneers (**Source 3**). The Rochdale Pioneers were dissatisfied with privately-owned shops which often swindled customers by

This engraving from the 1820s shows a member of the Associated Feltmakers – a hat-makers' friendly society – paying his subscription.

WE ASSIST EACH OTHER IN TIME OF NEED.

dishonest practices such as watering down milk or putting sand in sugar. They sold pure food at normal prices. Then they shared the *dividend* (profit) amongst customers in proportion to their purchases. Dividends could be left in the business to earn interest. This provided funds to help the store expand; by 1875 it had 8415 members.

Co-operative stores of this type soon spread throughout northern England and the industrial towns of Scotland. In close-knit communities they served as meeting places as well as shops. In 1863 a Co-operative Wholesale Society (CWS) was set up to buy goods cheaply in large quantities and supply co-op stores. By the 1870s the CWS was making its own goods, including soap, shoes and clothing.

## Craft unions

The failure of the Grand National Consolidated Trades Union, in 1834 (see page 64), left masses of poor, unskilled workers without union support. But it had much less effect on skilled craftsmen such as toolmakers, carpenters and bricklayers. Such men were essential to Britain's growing industries and not easy to replace. Consequently their small, local unions carried on bargaining for better pay and working conditions with some chance of success.

Like any other workers, craftsmen could gain advantages from organising on a large scale. This was shown in 1851 when over a hundred local trade societies of machinists, millwrights, engineers and toolmakers came together to form the Amalgamated Society of Engineers (ASE). After only nine months the ASE had 11,000 members and a permanent headquarters. Its members needed to be well paid to afford the weekly subscription

### SOURCE 3

The Rochdale Pioneers originally set out to do much more than run a store, as this statement of their aims shows (October 1844).

The objects and plans of this Society are …
The establishment of a store for the sale of provisions (food), clothing, etc.
Purchasing or erecting a number of houses, in which … members … may reside.
The manufacture of such articles as the Society may determine upon, for the employment of such members as may be without employment …
Purchase or rent [of] an estate or estates of land which shall be cultivated by the members who may be out of employment.

### QUESTIONS

1. Friendly societies have declined in importance since the nineteenth century. Why do you think this had happened?

2. Why do you think the Rochdale Pioneers wanted to provide houses for members (Source 3)?

3. Can you suggest a reason why the Rochdale Pioneers succeeded where earlier co-operatives had failed?

4. Why could the craft unions generally achieve their aims without calling strikes?

of 1 shilling (5p), at a time when most workers earned less than £1 a week. In return, they received benefits similar to those of friendly societies (**Source 5**).

The example of the ASE was soon followed in other skilled trades. During the 1850s and 60s, national craft unions were formed among carpenters and joiners, boilermakers, plasterers and others. Such unions preferred to settle their differences with employers round a table rather than strike. But if a stoppage was thought necessary they had sufficient funds to give strike pay to their members (**Source 6**). During the 1860s the ASE spent £26,000 on strike pay, compared with £450,000 on other benefits.

## Pickets and blacklegs

Not all the workers in a trade or craft would join the union. Indeed, in these years unionists were usually a minority in any group of workers. This could lead to bad feeling between union members and those who refused to join, especially during strikes when employers needed non-unionists to keep their businesses going. To run a successful strike, it was almost essential for union members to *picket* (guard) the entrance to the workplace and persuade non-unionists not to go to work. Such picketing sometimes led to scuffles and fights, even though it was illegal for pickets to 'molest' or 'obstruct' fellow workers.

In the Sheffield cutlery trade, in 1866, hostility between union members and non-members got out of hand. Unionists made several violent and murderous attacks on non-union men and *blacklegs* (those willing to work during a strike). In one incident a tin of gunpowder was exploded in the house of a non-unionist. The so-called 'Sheffield Outrages' gave trade unions a bad name, despite all the efforts of the craft unions to make them respectable.

In 1871 concern about union violence led Gladstone's Liberal government to outlaw picketing, even in its most peaceful form. This made effective strike action

SOURCE 7

Union members attacking the homes of 'blacklegs' who refuse to join a strike (from *Illustrated Midland News, 1870*). Such behaviour gave trade unions a bad name.

almost impossible. It took a change of government to get the decision reversed. Many working men in the towns had been given the vote in 1867 (see page 104). In 1874 these new electors helped to vote the Liberals out and the Conservatives in. Next year the new government, led by Benjamin Disraeli, repaid unionists by restoring the right to picket during a strike, provided they used only 'peaceful persuasion'.

## Organising the lower-paid

Craft unions like the ASE were for skilled workers – a minority of about one in ten of the working classes who had served an apprenticeship and learned a trade. Meanwhile most of the unskilled and semi-skilled did not belong to a union. Agricultural workers, inspired by Joseph Arch, a Warwickshire labourer, were organised into a national union in 1872 **(Source 8)**. But it was not until the late-1880s that the great mass of poorer workers began to form unions.

A series of successful strikes in London marked the turning point. In 1888 Annie Besant, a journalist, took up the cause of women working at Bryant and May's match factory. In articles for her weekly paper, *The Link*, she told of their dangerous work dipping matches in

SOURCE 8

In a book he wrote about his life, Joseph Arch here recalls the beginnings of the Agricultural Labourers' Union.

The day was February 7th 1872 ... My wife said, 'Joe, here's three men come to see you' ... They wanted to get the men together and start a union directly. I told them ... they would have to fight hard for it, and they would have to suffer a great deal; both they and their families. They said ... things could not be worse ... downright starvation lay before them unless the farmers could be made to raise their wages. Asking was of no use ... they must join together and strike ... When I saw that the men were in dead earnest ... I said I would address the meeting at 7 o'clock.

SOURCE 9

Some of the match girls at Bryant and May's who staged a successful strike in 1888.

phosphorus and condemned their low pay of a penny ($\frac{1}{2}$p) an hour. This led to a three-week stoppage by 700 match workers which forced the company to improve pay and conditions. In the next year London gas workers struck for an eight-hour day. Rather than let the lights go down in the capital, their employers soon gave in. This triumph was followed, days later, by a strike among London dockets that hit the headlines at home and abroad.

Loading and unloading ships at the docks was uncertain work. Most dockers were 'casual' labourers, hired to do a job by the hour and paid off when it was completed. Every morning thousands of men gathered at the gates of London's dockland, knowing that many of them would not get work that day (**Source 10**). Trouble flared up in August 1889 when men unloading dirty cargo asked for sixpence ($2\frac{1}{2}$p) an hour instead of the usual fivepence. When this was refused they walked out. Within three days they were joined by 10,000 strikers, all demanding a minimum wage of sixpence an hour – known as the 'docker's tanner' (**Source 11**).

The strikers were led by Ben Tillett, who had recently formed a small union of tea warehousemen. But the driving force behind the stoppage was John Burns, a big, broad-shouldered ship's engineer. Burns knew that for the strike to succeed it was necessary to prevent the employers bringing in men to do the strikers' work. He sent out pickets to patrol the docklands (**Source 13**). Burns also tried to gain public support by organising

---

**SOURCE 10**

Henry Mayhew was a journalist who wrote books about life in Victorian London. Here he describes the scene at a dock gate.

As the hour approaches eight, you know by the stream pouring through the gates … that the 'calling foremen' have made their appearance, and the 'casual men' are about to be taken on duty … Then begins the scuffling and scrambling, and stretching forth of countless hands high in the air, to catch the eye of him whose nod can give them work … Some men jump up on the backs of others … to attract his notice.

---

**SOURCE 11**

This view of casual dock workers comes from Colonel Birt, manager of London's Millwall Docks. The year was 1888.

Most of … these unfortunate fellows are without physical strength … miserably clad, scarcely with a boot on their foot … There are men who come on to work in our docks … without having a bit of food in their stomachs … They have worked for an hour, and have earned 5 pence ($2\frac{1}{2}$p); their hunger will not allow them to continue; they take the 5 pence in order that they may get food, perhaps the first food they have had for 24 hours.

---

**SOURCE 12**

The London Dock Strike of 1889: a procession of strikers leaving the East India Dock gates.

---

marches of ragged, half-starved dockers through the streets of London. Bands played, banners were held aloft, and fish-heads and rotting vegetables put on sticks to show what dockers had to live on.

At first the employers stood firm, confident of being able to starve the strikers into surrender. But growing public sympathy for the dockers led to money pouring in from other unions, church organisations, sports clubs and even from workers in Australia who raised the enormous sum of £30,000. After five weeks, the employers realised they were beaten and granted the strikers' main demands. The victorious union was now firmly established.

The 'docker's tanner' was a victory not just for dockers but for lower-paid workers generally. They were encouraged to form new and powerful unions, some on a national basis; the General Railway Workers' Union and the Miners' Federation of Great Britain were both founded in 1889. The new unions were much less willing to co-operate with employers than the older craft unions. 'It is the work of the trade unionist', wrote Ben Tillett, 'to stamp out poverty from the land'. Consequently there were many long and bitter strikes in the years ahead. Progress in organising the lower-paid boosted the total membership of trade unions from 750,000 in 1888 to 2 million in 1900.

## Parliamentary reform – 'the leap in the dark'

Voting rights were still based on wealth and ownership of property after the 1832 Reform Act (see page 60). However by the 1860s there was growing support, in and out of Parliament, for a further widening of the *franchise* (the right to vote) to include skilled tradesmen. A National Reform League, backed by many MPs, held meetings all over Britain, including a big demonstration in Hyde Park, London, in 1866. The government tried to prevent the meeting in the Park but crowds

removed nearly a mile of railings. Parliament had recently defeated a Reform Bill; a new Conservative government, led by Lord Derby, now felt obliged to try again.

A LEAP IN THE DARK.

SOURCE 15

This cartoon appeared in *Punch* magazine at the time of the 1867 Reform Act. It shows 'Britannia' (Britain) being carried into a thick hedge (reform).

SOURCE 16

An election using the new secret ballot was reported in the *Times* on 14 September 1872.

Usually an election day here has been a day of great political tumult and uproar. But today … when the poll opened the principal streets of the town were almost as quiet as usual … Some working men … seemed to have no proper idea at all of the ballot ; odd ones of them would, on entering the booth, ask the constable at the door where they had to tell the name of the candidate they wanted to vote for … One or two cases of personations (trying to vote in another person's name) were early reported, but the guilty parties made a clear escape.

SOURCE 17

The arrival of the newly elected Keir Hardie at the House of Commons (August 1892) was reported in the *Morning Post* as follows.

Mr Keir Hardie drove up to the House in a toil-stained working suit with a cloth cap on his head and accompanied by a noisy brass band followed by a noisy and disreputable throng from the dockside slums which included many undesirable foreign elements who should be driven from our shores before they infect our good and sensible working men with their bloodthirsty beliefs.

The resulting second Parliamentary Reform Act (1867) created nearly one million new voters – mostly better-off workers in the towns – and doubled the overall size of the electorate. All male householders in the boroughs now had the franchise. In addition, 45 seats were taken from small boroughs and given to growing towns and the larger counties. No one could be sure what the effects of the wider franchise would be. Lord Derby called the Act 'a leap in the dark'. Certainly it opened the way to further reform.

In 1872 the corrupt system of open voting was replaced by secret ballot. This stopped the bribing of electors because now there was no way of telling which way a man voted (**Source 16**). The last major parliamentary reform of the nineteenth century, in 1884, gave the vote to male householders in the counties. As a result, a further $2\frac{1}{2}$ million men were added to the electorate. The 1884 Act was passed only after a fierce struggle in the House of Lords, where many great landowners objected to their farm workers having the vote.

### The origins of the Labour Party

After 1884, almost half the voters were working-class. Yet the policies of the main parties, Liberal and Conservative, still favoured the better-off. Many of the new voters felt it was time they had a political party to advance their interests. The first working-class MPs were two miners, Alexander McDonald and Thomas Burt, elected in 1874. At that time MPs were not

James Keir Hardie (1856 – 1915) dressed in the manner which shocked fellow MP's in the House of Commons.

paid, so they had to be supported by union funds. McDonald and Burt sat with the Liberals in Parliament but they were usually called 'Labour' or 'Lib-Lab'. By 1885 there were 11 'Lib-Labs', but still little prospect of either the Liberals or Conservatives carrying out social reforms of the kind working people wanted.

In this extract from his book, *Merrie England* (1895), Robert Blatchford, a member of the Independent Labour Party, describes his vision of socialism for Britain.

I would make all the land, mills, mines, factories, works, shops, ships and railways the property of the people ... I would institute public dining halls, public baths, public wash-houses on the best plans, and so set free the hands of those slaves – our English women ... I would have all our children fed and clothed and educated at the cost of the state ... I would have the people become their own artists, actors, musicians, soldiers and police.

The playwright George Bernard Shaw belonged to the Fabian Society, a middle-class group supporting socialism. Writing in 1893, he explains how the trade unions could finance a Labour party.

The establishment of a great number of unions in formerly unorganised trades has trebled the numbers ... of the trade union organisation ... The money difficulty does not exist for unions. A penny a week from every member of a trade union would produce £300,000. This shows how easily the larger unions could provide £30,000 to finance 50 Labour candidates at £600 a piece.

Keir Hardie, a Scottish miner, was elected MP for West Ham, in London's dockland, in 1892. Hardie refused to be a 'Lib-Lab' and would have nothing to do with the existing parties. To show his independence, he turned up at the House dressed in a deerstalker hat and working clothes instead of the top hat and tailcoat worn by MPs in those days (**Source 17**). Next year Hardie took the lead in forming the Independent Labour Party (ILP). Its policies were based on *socialism* – the belief that the state rather than private owners should control the country's main sources of wealth, including key industries, for the benefit of all (**Source 19**).

The ILP suffered a crushing election defeat in 1895 when all 28 of its candidates lost, including Hardie. There seemed little chance of success without the official support and financial backing of the trade unions (**Source 20**). A Trades Union Congress (TUC) had been formed back in 1868 to bring unions together to discuss matters of common interest. The TUC was persuaded to set up a Labour Representation Committee in 1900 and start a fund to pay candidates' election expenses as well as the salaries of any who became MPs. In 1906, after the Committee's candidates had won 29 seats in an election, it changed its name to the Labour Party.

### QUESTIONS

1. In Source 15, who are the hunters meant to represent? What seems to be their attitude to the leaping horse?

2. Why did the voters mentioned in Source 16 think they had to 'tell' the name of the candidate of their choice?

3. Why do you think Robert Blatchford (Source 19) believed it necessary for children not only to be educated but also fed and clothed at the cost of the state?

4. Why were the trade unions so closely involved in the growth of the Labour party?

# Assessment tasks

## A Knowledge and understanding

1 Make a timeline to summarise improvements in the position of working-class people between 1840 and 1900. Include not just events in particular years but also things that happened over longer periods of time. Divide your timeline into two columns headed 'better-off workers' and 'the low paid' (some entries will belong in both columns).

2 What were the most important consequences of the 1889 London dock strike, (a) immediately, and (b) in the longer term?

3 a Working-class householders in towns got the vote before those in the country. Can you suggest any reasons for this?

 b What do you think Lord Derby was worried about when he called the 1867 Reform Act 'a leap in the dark'?

## B Interpretations and sources

4 Here are two modern views of the 1889 London dock strike.

By winning this massive, unexpected and surprising strike a lot more than a 'tanner' was won ... What a miracle ... that a strike that was won by mass picketing, with trains of scab labour (non-union workers) sent back from the main line stations, saw no overt (open) violence to damage the obvious public sympathy.
(Ron Todd, General Secretary of the Transport and General Workers' Union, 1988)

Burns knew that blacklegs must be discouraged at any cost, physical or otherwise ... Very real terror reigned in dockland. 'Men have left their work ... being unable to enter or leave the docks in safety', wrote a labourer to the press ... This was the side of the struggle on which neither Burns nor Tillett wanted too much limelight.
(Colonel O.B. Oram, former Superintendent of Surrey Commercial Docks, 1964)

 a Can you account for the differences between these views?

 b Which view do you find the more convincing, and why?

5 Sources 12, 16 and 17 are taken from newspapers. In each, what is the writer's attitude towards the events being described?

6 What do the sources in this chapter tell you about the differing aims and methods of (a) craftsmen's unions, and (b) unions for the lower paid?

# 11 Arts and pastimes

## Victorian arts and popular culture

William Blake, in his poem *Jerusalem* (1804), described the new factories as 'dark Satanic mills', spoiling England's 'green and pleasant land'. Many people, horrified at the industrial changes going on around them, felt the same. Factories were ugly, dirty and noisy. Coal mines, growing in size and number, scarred the landscape with their slag-heaps. Later the coming of railways tore great gaps through town and countryside.

### Escaping into the past

It was not surprising that this world of clanking machines, belching smoke and hissing steam led some people to look back longingly to a time when Britain had been a quieter, prettier place. Poets increasingly wrote about the beauties of nature, which now seemed under threat from smoke, dust and brickwork. Some novelists set their stories in previous ages, mixing imaginary characters with real people and historical events.

Architects, above all, took their inspiration from the past. They designed buildings, from town halls to railway stations, with towers and turrets – in the style of the castles and cathedrals of the Middle Ages **(Source 1)**. Well known examples of such architecture in London include the present Houses of Parliament, built in the 1830s to replace the old buildings destroyed by fire, and Tower Bridge, opened in 1894. Large structures of this kind were easier to build once cheap, mass-produced iron and steel became available.

Painters too looked back into history. One group set out to copy the styles of medieval Italian painting; they chose subjects from the Bible and from poems

**SOURCE 1**

St Pancras railway station and hotel, London, built in 1868 – an example of Victorian architecture in the medieval style. The architect, George Gilbert Scott, also designed the Albert Memorial in Kensington Gardens, which earned him a knighthood.

about beautiful maidens and knights in shining armour **(Source 2)**. However one great English painter was prepared to paint the new industrial world. J.M.W. Turner painted a steamship in a storm and also 'Rain, steam, speed', a picture of a steam train crossing a viaduct. These seemed strange subjects to some people; a critic described the railway scene as 'one of Mr Turner's little jokes'.

## Views of industry and empire

Many Victorian writers showed concern for the world around them – and none more so than Charles Dickens (1812–70), the most famous novelist of his time. His stories are set mainly in London and the South-East. They expose many of the evils of the age – the horrors of slum life, the sufferings of children, the misery caused by harsh laws and unfeeling officials. One of the best known, *Hard Times*, is set in a northern factory town – Preston in Lancashire – which Dickens called 'Coketown'. The book attacks inhuman factory conditions **(Source 3)** as well as condemning methods of schooling which made pupils learn 'facts' they did not understand.

Some of the best writers – and keenest readers – of Victorian novels were women. Elizabeth Gaskell (1810–65) lived most of her life in Manchester and wrote a number of novels set against a background of Lancashire factory life. In *North and South* she compared life in northern industrial areas with that in the largely unspoilt southern counties. Another woman, Mary Ann Evans (1819–80), writing under the pen-name George Eliot, also chose serious subjects. One of her novels, *Felix Holt*, is set against the struggle for the 1867 Reform Bill (see page 104).

**SOURCE 3**

Charles Dickens wrote *Hard Times* after visiting Preston in 1853. Here is part of his description of the place he called 'Coketown'.

It was a town of machinery and tall chimneys … It had a black canal in it, and a river that ran purple with ill-smelling dye, and vast piles of building full of windows where there was a rattling and trembling all day long, and where the piston of the steam-engine worked monotonously up and down, like the head of an elephant in a state of melancholy (sad) madness … The measured motion of [the engines'] shadows on the walls was the substitute Coketown had to show for the shadows of rustling woods; while, for the summer hum of insects, it could offer, all the year round … the whirr of shafts and wheels.

| QUESTIONS | |
|---|---|
| **1** | Source 1 was designed to contrast with most industrial styles of building. How was this achieved? |
| **2** | Where in Source 3 does Dickens, like Blake, recall a quieter, prettier England? |
| **3** | Can you think of a reason why Mary Ann Evans wrote under a man's name? |
| **4** | According to Kipling in Source 4, what were the hardships suffered by soldiers guarding the empire? |

Later in the century, writers took an interest in the expanding empire. Rudyard Kipling was born in India and spent some of his early years there. He wrote popular verse about 'Tommy Atkins' – a nickname for the British soldier – and expressed sympathy for the hard and unrewarding life of a soldier. Kipling's stories show an understanding of Indian ways and customs, but he also boasted of Britain's mission to rule 'lesser breeds' within her empire (**Source 4**). Young readers were inspired to take a pride in the empire by writers such as G.A. Henty. Many of Henty's heroes fought battles in foreign lands (**Source 5**).

## Public houses and music halls

Throughout Victorian times, 'respectable' men and women campaigned against the evils of alcohol. So-called *temperance* reformers were against even moderate drinking. They said people should abstain from (give up) the 'demon drink' altogether. Total abstinence, or *totalism*, was their slogan, and because one temperance speaker had a stutter in this became *teetotalism*!

Despite all the talk of misery and hardship caused by excessive drinking, the Victorian working classes spent much of their free time in public houses. Beer was regarded as 'manly' and spirits were a useful pain-killer. Victorian pubs, although bare and cheerless by today's standards,

### SOURCE 4

In this famous poem, Rudyard Kipling (1865–1936) takes it for granted that white men were born to rule. He also sees guarding the empire as a thankless task for British soldiers.

Take up the White Man's burden –
Send forth the best ye breed –
Go, bind your sons to exile
To serve your captives' need;
To wait in heavy harness
On fluttered folk and wild –
Your new-caught, sullen peoples,\
Half-devil and half-child …
Take up the White Man's burden –
And reap his old reward;
The blame of those ye better,
The hate of those ye guard.

### SOURCE 5

One of G. A. Henty's heroic empire stories. Cabul (now usually spelt Kabul) is the capital of Afghanistan, a mountainous country between India and Russia. General Roberts, later to win fame in the Boer War, led victorious British forces there in the years 1878 – 80.

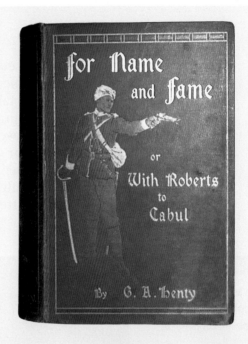

### SOURCE 6

This cartoon, published in 1886, contrasts the evils of drink with the benefits of reading books. 'Temperance' reformers, who were against drinking, hoped libraries would lure people away from public houses.

THE RIVALS: WHICH SHALL IT BE?

Music halls appeal to a far larger class of pleasure seekers than theatres. Prices are not high, and the entertainment provided does not, as a rule, demand an undivided attention. You can smoke and drink at your ease while the entertainment is going on, for a ledge fixed at the back of the seat of the man in front of you serves as a table on which to place your glass … Hence the 'halls' are especially favoured by young men. But … in the East End of London and south of the Thames many will take their wives and children or sweethearts.

were luxurious compared with most working-class homes. The friendly 'local' became an entertainment centre, with gambling, singing and games like dominoes and shove ha'penny. Pubs also became bases for organising outdoor games, once shorter working hours meant a free Saturday afternoon. Football and cricket teams often used a pub as a changing room.

Out of pub sing-songs and recitals grew the music hall, a place where audiences could drink and smoke as they enjoyed the 'turns' of comedians, singers, dancers and acrobats (**Source 7**). By the 1890s music halls could be found in every town; London had around thirty. Nearly all music hall performers came from working-class backgrounds. One of the greatest, a singer called Marie Lloyd, earned £100 a week – a fortune at that time.

Music halls were forbidden by law from putting on plays. These could only be performed in a theatre, where drinking and smoking were restricted to a bar area at the back. Theatre-goers were anxious to prevent the spread of 'music hall habits' into theatres at a time when smoking tobacco, rather than taking it as snuff, was becoming fashionable. Most smokers used a pipe, but soldiers shipped to the Black Sea to fight in the Crimean War against Russia (1854–6) helped to popularise the Turkish habit of smoking cigars and cigarettes.

**SOURCE 8**

The audience at a popular music hall in Lambeth, London.

Artist's impression of 'The Derby' at Epsom racecourse in 1853. First run in 1780, the Derby is one of the oldest events in the horseracing calendar.

## The growth of 'spectator sport'

Prize-fighting and horse-racing were the most popular spectator sports in the early nineteenth century. There was heavy gambling on both. Race meetings were attended by the highest and lowest in the land; royalty, lords and ladies had to keep their distance from tradesmen, ruffians and thieves. Similarly, spectators from all classes of society assembled in their thousands to watch contests between famous bare-knuckle fighters. Bad injuries sometimes resulted from such fights, which could last for hours. It was not until 1867 that the rules which now govern the sport were drawn up by the eighth Marquis of Queensberry.

Other old sports took on their modern form during Victorian times. Organised cricket had been played by village teams since the 1700s. English county clubs were founded in the mid-nineteenth century and the first County Championship was held in 1873. By then the British had introduced the game in many parts of the empire. All the major Test teams of today come from countries once ruled by Britain. The first Test Match was played between men of Australia and England in 1877, at Melbourne, Australia.

This report of a women's cricket match appeared in the *British Register* for October 1811.

A grand cricket match has been played this month between eleven women of Surrey and eleven women of Hampshire for 500 guineas (£525). The combatants (players) were dressed in loose trousers with short fringed petticoats descending to the knees and light flannel waistcoats with sashes round the waist. The performers were all ages and sizes, from fourteen years upwards to fifty.

Women also played cricket (**Source 10**). There are records of ladies' matches going back to 1745, although the first women's cricket club, the White Heather, was formed in 1887. Earlier, the change from under-arm to over-arm bowling is said to have been pioneered by a woman. Christina Willes, when practising with her brother, found under-arm bowling difficult because of her long skirts. So she bowled over-arm and her brother managed to get the rules changed in 1835.

Football was for many years a mixture of rugby and soccer. But when the Football Association was formed in 1863 – by ex-public schoolboys from Eton and Harrow – one of its rules banned handling the ball. Players who objected to this restriction broke away to form rugby clubs. The Rugby Union was founded in 1873. In 1895 the Northern Union, later known as the Rugby League, went its own way after some clubs hired paid professionals. By then, professional teams were common in 'Association football' (**Source 11**). The F.A. Cup competition began in 1871. Thirty years later, a crowd of 110,000 – larger than any British soccer crowd of recent years – saw the final in the grounds of Crystal Palace in south London.

The movement of such large numbers of people was made possible by the railways. Cheap excursion trains not only carried sporting crowds but also took some of the better paid working-class families on day trips and holidays by the sea. An annual week's holiday, usually without pay, was common by the late-nineteenth century, especially in the Midlands and North. Those unable to afford a week away often saved for a day trip, especially after the Bank Holidays Act of 1871. This fixed four weekdays in the year in England (five in Scotland) when the banks would be closed. As it was difficult to do business without the banks, these soon became public holidays for all.

It is quite odd to see how strongly the people in League districts are smitten by the football fever … Youths and young men patronise the excursion trains to fields of combat 50 or 100 miles from home … in their workaday dirt, and with their workaday adjectives very loose on their tongues … At Bolton a worthy town councillor, who chanced to die during the football season, was, at his dying request, carried to the grave by four of the team.

In the essentials of Christianity – the feelings of brotherly and neighbourly love and kindness, and the virtue of patience – the working classes are not lacking. Their non-attendance at places of worship … and the reasons for it are simple and not far to seek … Sermons are, as a rule … dull … [Also] Sunday being the only day the working classes have entirely to themselves, they require it for rest and fresh air … But the reason most frequently given … is that they have not clothes good enough to go in.

## Declining church attendance

The Christian religion remained strong among well-to-do Victorian families. On Sundays, most middle-class people went to church or chapel at least once, while in the strictest households family prayers and Bible-readings took the place of games and entertainments. The Methodists and Evangelicals (see Chapter 5) were still dedicated to helping the less fortunate. Dr Barnardo's East End Mission to care for London's homeless children (1867) and William Booth's Salvation Army (1878) showed how

QUESTIONS

**1** What clues are there in Sources 10 and 11 that cricket and football appealed to different classes in society?

**2** How did changes in public and personal transport affect people's leisure activities in the late 1800s?

**3** Can you suggest reasons why churches were better attended in country areas than in towns and cities?

**4** In Source 14, what seems to be the attitude of the cartoonist towards Darwin?

SOURCE 14

This Victorian cartoon, portraying Charles Darwin as a monkey, is entitled 'As others see us'.

seriously some Christians took their responsibilities towards the poor.

In country areas, churches were still well attended and parish life flourished. However in towns and cities the mass of the people were indifferent or even hostile towards organised religion – especially the Church of England, which was thought to be for the well-to-do. Only the Methodists and Catholics had any real support among industrial workers. Working-class people had little free time and many did not see why they should spend their only day of rest in church (**Source 13**). This did not necessarily mean that they were unbelievers. Many still prayed to God and used churches for baptisms, marriages and funerals.

Meanwhile, some of the basic ideas and beliefs of the Churches were coming under attack. For centuries Christians had accepted the exact word of the Bible, believing its writers had been inspired by God. But scientific discoveries were casting doubt upon some Biblical statements. In 1830 Charles Lyell, a geologist, claimed that the earth had developed through millions of years of *evolution* (gradual change). If this were true, the earth could not have been created in six days, as described in the Book of Genesis.

A more serious challenge to the old beliefs came in 1859, when Charles Darwin published his *Origin of Species*.

This claimed that living creatures too had evolved over millions of years, from one original form of life which may have been a simple cell. The idea that the human race had not been created separately but had developed from an ape-like creature horrified many Christians. For nearly thirty years a battle raged between Christians attacking Darwin's theory and scientists defending it. The argument also divided young and old (**Source 15**).

SOURCE 15

Writing in 1916, E.R. Pease, a founder member of the Labour Party, recalled how in his youth the evolution debate had divided families.

*The Origin of Species* ... separated the young generation of that period from their parents ... The older folk as a rule refused to accept or to consider the new doctrine ... The young men of the time grew up with the new ideas and accepted them as a matter of course ... Our parents ... lived in a world which bore no relation to our own ... because they knew no evolution ... We could accept nothing on trust from those who still believed that the early chapters of Genesis accurately described the origin of the universe.

Eventually most people came to see that scientific discoveries need not destroy belief in God and that a person could be a Christian without accepting every word of the Bible as fact. Even so, the debate about evolution shook the foundations of Victorian religion. By the end of the century the Church's hold upon the people had begun to loosen. Fewer attended church services and activities on Sundays were less strictly controlled. Such changes came slowly at first; it was only after World War One (1914–18) that the decline of Christianity in Britain accelerated.

## The rise of the popular press

By the 1880s free schooling for all children (see page 123) was creating a wider reading public. However, many working-class people found newspapers such as the *Times* and *Morning Post* boring and difficult to understand. These papers catered for a small, well educated readership. George Newnes, manager of a fancy goods store, saw the need for a paper written in simple language with short paragraphs. In 1881 he started *Tit-Bits* which consisted entirely of brief items of information and news **(Source 16)**.

Alfred Harmsworth, one of Newnes's office workers, decided to copy his employer. In 1888 he started *Answers to Correspondents*, a magazine containing replies to readers' questions. The first issue included articles on 'What the Queen eats' and 'How to cure freckles'. To boost sales, Harmsworth offered his readers a prize of £1 a week for life if they could guess correctly the value of gold held in the vaults of the Bank of England. Profits from this competition allowed Harmsworth to start a boys' magazine called *Comic Cuts*.

By 1896 Harmsworth could afford to launch the first popular British daily paper, the *Daily Mail*. Its sales soon reached a million copies a day. The *Mail* did not report parliamentary debates in detail as the old-style papers did. Instead it offered prize competitions, sports news, fashion, gossip and 'human interest' stories. Lord Salisbury, prime minister at the time, dismissed the *Mail* as a newspaper 'written by office-boys for office-boys'. But it set Harmsworth on a career which brought him riches, fame and honours. In his later years he was made Lord Northcliffe – the first of the 'press barons'.

---

**SOURCE 16**

*Tit-Bits*, in its first issue on 22 October 1881, introduced itself to its readers as follows.

*Tit-Bits* ... will be a production of all that is most interesting in the books, periodicals and newspapers of this and other countries ... Any person who takes in *Tit-Bits* for three months will at the end of that time be an entertaining companion, as he will then have at his command a stock of smart sayings ... It will be the business of the conductors of *Tit-Bits* to find ... the best things that have ever been said or written, and weekly to place them before the public for one penny.

---

**SOURCE 17**

Alfred Harmsworth, later Lord Northcliffe (1865 – 1922) pictured in 1897 reading a copy of his best-selling *Daily Mail*.

---

# Assessment tasks

## A Knowledge and understanding

1 How would the growth of the popular pastimes described in this chapter have been assisted by (a) better pay for many workers, (b) shorter working hours, and (c) education for all?

2 a Describe the challenges facing the Christian Churches in the nineteenth century as a result of (i) changes in industry and society, and (ii) the progress of science.

   b In what ways did Christians respond to these challenges, and how successful were they?

3 Search for evidence of Victorian leisure pursuits in your area. Things to look for include nineteenth-century public houses, converted theatres and music halls, lending libraries and Victorian structures at sporting venues and seaside resorts.

## B Interpretations and sources

4 Here are some views on Alfred Harmsworth (Lord Northcliffe) and his *Daily Mail*.

Originally, apart from a born zest for news, he was only interested in newspapers as bringing money. Later he appreciated them also as bringing power. He never appreciated that they brought responsibility .... His papers ... assumed a mass of readers ... who would never know or care if half the serious news were left out ... Provided it gave them the excitements that they wanted they troubled little about its veracity (truth).
(R.C. K. Ensor, 1936)

The 'quality' press held a low opinion of the lively *Daily Mail*... Yet Harmsworth must be given credit for being the first daily journalist to address a large section of the .... lower middle class. The 'serious' journals looked down upon this important audience ... their journalism was too intellectual, too heavy.
(Donald Read, 1979)

A few years ago, I saw a *Daily Mail* leading page for a day in 1908 ... I noticed that a whole column ... was devoted to an account of Elgar's First Symphony. Now no popular newspaper today would give so much space to a new piece of music .... Did Northcliffe believe ... that he had a certain duty towards his readers, so that he could not ignore a major work by Elgar? .... I am inclined to think that ... he was not entirely without a sense of cultural responsibility.
(J. B. Priestley, 1970)

   a What do these accounts agree and disagree about?

   b What is the attitude of each writer towards Harmsworth?

   c Why are disagreements of this kind very hard to resolve?

5 Look carefully at Source 6.

   a How does the artist make the library seem the better place?

   b Was the choice presented here a real one for most working people?

   c Do you think this drawing would have had the desired effect? Give reasons for your answer.

   d Compare the architecture in the drawing with Source 1.

6 What does Source 15 tell you about (a) the evolution 'debate' in Victorian times, and (b) its effect upon people's attitudes and relationships?

# Poverty and progress

## Social changes in Victorian Britain

The Industrial Revolution made Britain, for a time, the richest country on earth. But the price of material progress was misery and squalor for millions of men, women and children. In 1890, William Booth, founder of the Salvation Army, published a book called *In Darkest England* which urged the British to think less about empire-building overseas and more about the problem of poverty on their own doorstep. Booth believed that the true 'white man's burden' lay not in 'darkest Africa' but among the wretched slum-dwellers of Britain's industrial towns **(Source 1)**.

### Life below the poverty line

'How many', Booth wondered, 'dwell in Darkest England?' He guessed at a figure of three million – roughly a tenth of the total population at that time. But things were far worse than he thought. A book published in 1889 claimed to provide a scientific answer to this question. It was

### SOURCE 1

Here is an extract from William Booth's book, *In Darkest England and the Way Out*. The term 'darkest Africa' was used by a famous explorer of the African interior, H.M. Stanley.

As there is a darkest Africa, is there not also a darkest England? … The foul and fetid (stinking) breath of our slums is almost as poisonous as that of the African swamp. Fever is almost as chronic there as on the Equator … A population sodden with drink, steeped in vice, eaten up by every social and physical malady (disorder), these are the … [inhabitants] of Darkest England … to whose rescue I would now summon all that is best in the manhood and womanhood of our land.

### SOURCE 2

Slum-dwellers in London photographed in 1889.

the first of seventeen volumes on *The Life and Labour of the People of London*, produced by a wealthy ship owner, Charles Booth (no relation to William). With a team of researchers, Charles Booth had spent three years doing social surveys which showed that a third of all London's families lived in deep poverty, on about £1 a week or less **(Source 3)**.

Critics of Charles Booth's work said London was exceptional. But in 1899 Seebohm Rowntree, one of the chocolate-making family, carried out a house-to-house survey in York, with similar results. Like Booth, Rowntree calculated a 'poverty line' based on the minimum amount of food, clothing and fuel people needed to stay healthy. He found that 28 per cent of York's population fell below the line. Some were in poverty through idleness, heavy drinking or gambling. But by far the most common causes of poverty were low wages and unemployment.

If these findings were true of Britain as a whole, over 10 million people were so poor that they lacked, in Rowntree's words, 'some of the necessities of a civilised life'. Many families could only afford to rent one room. Their diet may have contained enough bulk to satisfy hunger, but it was short of nourishing food. 'If there's anything extra to buy', said a woman in the York survey, 'such as a

pair of boots for one of the children, me and the children goes without dinner.'

Charles Booth showed that on earnings of about 30 shillings (£1.50) per week a worker could feed his family well most days. Such *artisans* (skilled tradesmen) usually dressed tidily and lived in solidly built houses. The better-paid artisans were even able to put money in a post office savings bank. Booth concluded that for many families 10 shillings (50p) a week marked the difference between poverty and 'solid working-class comfort'.

## Wealth and privilege

At the other end of the social scale, the *aristocrats* or upper class were still very rich and powerful. One Scottish lord, the Duke of Sutherland, owned the entire

### SOURCE 4

A poor country family in the 1860s. Farm labourers were the lowest paid of all workers, so poverty was not confined to the towns. Throughout the Victorian Age, the population of the countryside declined through emigration overseas and a steady drift to the towns.

SOURCE 5

Frances Greville, later Countess of Warwick, here describes her life among the aristocracy in the late-nineteenth century.

The men went out shooting after breakfast and then came the emptiness of the long morning from which I suffered silently … After a large luncheon, finishing up with coffee and liqueurs, the women … would spend the time until the men returned for tea changing their clothes … We changed our clothes four times a day at least. This kept our maids and ourselves extraordinarily busy … The hours between tea and dinner … used often to be sheer boredom, until seven when we went off to dress for dinner.

county of Sutherland. Lord Hertford's properties included farms, mines, quarries, parts of towns and a castle in Wales he had never seen! In the late-1800s about half the Cabinet (the senior government ministers) still belonged to the House of Lords.

From their lands, most members of the upper class received a large income without having to spend their time earning it. This meant they could, if they wished, devote themselves to pleasure – hunting, shooting, yachting, gambling on horses or holidaying abroad. When they were not entertaining guests on their country estates they went to live in their town houses and enjoyed London 'society'. For some, however, the endless round of activity was often just an escape from boredom (Source 5).

The Industrial Revolution did nothing to narrow the gap between rich and poor. However it did increase the number of *middle classes* in between. A few factory owners, bankers and other businessmen became rich enough to copy the aristocracy. They bought land and built mansions staffed with butlers, cooks, housemaids and gardeners. In the 1870s four-fifths of all land in the United Kingdom was owned by fewer than 7000 people.

Members of the 'professions' – including accountants, lawyers, architects, doctors and senior government officials – were also increasing in wealth and numbers. They lived in large houses with spacious gardens and often sent their sons to the same expensive boarding schools as the aristocracy. The *lower* middle class of office workers, shopkeepers and small businessmen only had modest incomes, but they usually managed to employ at

SOURCE 6

A middle-class family group photographed in the late-1800s.

**QUESTIONS**

1. What factors make it difficult to calculate a 'poverty line' that can be applied to all families?

2. What does Source 5 suggest about relationships between upper class men and women?

3. Can you suggest reasons why the expansion of industry led to an increase in the number of 'middle class' occupations?

4. How would household chores have been different in the 1800s, before ordinary homes had electricity?

least one maidservant. People were more prepared to spend their money on domestic help in the days before washing machines, vacuum cleaners and modern heating appliances.

## Public health

In Victorian times, governments did not consider it their business to help families living in poverty. There was no Social Security for unemployed, sick or old people – just the dreaded parish workhouse. But although Parliament ignored *individual* hardship, it did come to accept the need to improve working and living conditions for the mass of the people. Acts were passed to protect women and children in factories and mines (see pages 41 and 54). Then, after the deadly disease of cholera spread from Asia to Britain's slum areas in the 1830s, governments became concerned with public health standards.

In 1842 Edwin Chadwick, Secretary of the Poor Law Commission, published a *Report on the Sanitary Condition of the Labouring Population* which caused great alarm. It produced evidence from nationwide surveys to show that hundreds of thousands of families lived in filthy, damp and unventilated houses, without proper drainage, sewerage or water supply. Slums of this kind were breeding grounds of disease **(Source 8)**. Chadwick argued that ill-health resulting from poor living conditions was a direct cause of poverty. He said it was better to take preventive action than to spend money on poor relief when the damage was done.

Chadwick wanted the government to take responsibility for improving public health. It took a severe outbreak of cholera in 1847 to spur ministers into action. The first Public Health Act (1848) set up a Board of Health in London with the power to create local boards around the country. These controlled necessary services such as cleansing, draining and paving the streets. But a town was not required to do anything unless it had an unusually high death-rate. In practice, only a sixth of the population was served by a local health board.

Not until 1875 did a government attempt any large-scale improvements. In that year a Public Health Act set up a nationwide system of sanitary authorities responsible for sewerage, refuse disposal and water supply. Medical officers of health and sanitary inspectors also had to be appointed in all areas. By 1900 most of the basic sanitary services had been established and British towns were much cleaner and healthier. On average, people could expect to live ten years longer than in 1850. The public health problem had now become largely a housing problem.

Lower-paid workers could not afford the rents of even the cheapest houses. They

### SOURCE 8

Here is an extract from Edwin Chadwick's famous Report.

Disease, wherever its attacks are frequent, is always found in connection with ... damp and filth, and close and overcrowded dwellings ... and where those circumstances are removed by drainage, proper cleansing, better ventilation ... the frequency of such disease is abated (lessened) ... For all these purposes better supplies of water are absolutely necessary ... The annual loss of life from filth and bad ventilation is greater than the loss from death or wounds in any wars in which the country has been engaged in modern times.

Richard Cross was the government minister responsible for the Artisans' Dwelling Act. During a parliamentary debate in 1875 he explained one of the main aims of the Act.

I take it as a starting point that it is not the duty of the Government to provide … citizens with any of the necessaries of life … [Yet] no one will doubt the right of the State to interfere in matters relating to sanitary laws … Health is actually wealth … If we can prevent waste of life, power, energy … and everything that makes a nation healthy and wealthy, it is our duty to interfere and see whether we cannot do something to arrest this waste.

Slum housing in Glasgow in the late-1800s.

had no choice but to rent a single room or share with other families. An Artisans' Dwellings Act of 1875 gave local councils power to take over and clear whole slum areas (**Source 9**). In places such as London and Birmingham prompt action was taken. But private builders redeveloped the cleared sites and let their houses to better-off workers. Slum clearance alone would not improve the living standards of poor families; the slums needed to be replaced by homes within the reach of the lower-paid. Little progress was made in this direction before the 1920s.

## Schools for the poor

There were great differences in education between Scotland and England. In Scotland most villages had their own schools, paid for out of local rates, as early as 1700. These taught children from the poorest families as well as those of the *lairds* (landowners). Consequently not just well-to-do Scots were educated. 'You cannot ordinarily find a *servant* in Scotland but he can read or write', said Daniel Defoe, writing in the early 1700s. Things were very different in England and Wales. Until the late-1800s many working-class children were denied education because their parents were unable to pay for it.

In some parts of England the Churches had been raising money to provide free schools for the poor since the seventeenth century. But even where such charity schools existed, many parents preferred to keep their children at work to add to the family income. Sunday schools were more popular in the new industrial areas because they allowed children to get some education without giving up the chance to earn money.

In the early 1800s, the two main church societies running free schools for the poor used a 'monitorial system' of teaching. The teacher gave a lesson to a group of older pupils – the 'monitors' – and they passed it on to the juniors. Such methods were almost worthless. The pupils were drilled to reply to set questions with answers they often did not understand **(Source 11)**. Not all working-class education was provided by the Churches. Some children attended 'dame schools' – so called because they were usually run by women. Any person, no matter how ignorant, could set up a school in their home and charge a few pence a week.

In all kinds of schools for poor children the curriculum was usually limited to religious knowledge and the 'three Rs' (reading, 'riting and 'rithmetic). Pupils

## QUESTIONS

**1** What was the main advantage of the 'monitorial system' so far as the providers of schooling were concerned?

**2** In what ways is the room shown in Source 12 ill-equipped for teaching children?

**3** Why was the teaching in Joseph Ashby's school (Source 13) restricted to reading, writing and arithmetic?

**4** What effect would large classes like the one shown in Source 15 have had upon teaching methods?

### SOURCE 11

This example of the 'question and answer' method of teaching comes from *The Child's Guide to Knowledge, by a Lady* – a popular textbook used in schools throughout the Victorian period.

| | |
|---|---|
| Question | Who made the world? |
| Answer | The great and good God. |
| Question | Are there not many things in it you would like to know about? |
| Answer | Yes, very much. |
| Question | Pray then what is bread made of? |
| Answer | Flour. |
| Question | What is flour? |
| Answer | Wheat ground into powder by the miller. |
| Question | What injury is wheat liable to? |
| Answer | To three kinds of diseases, called blight, mildew and smut. |

were taught to fear God and not to try to rise above their station in life. Parliament voted its first grant for education – £20,000 to the church societies – in 1833. Such grants increased from year to year as concern grew about the large number of British workers who could not read and write. Britain's chief trading rivals in Europe and North America were developing systems of education which left their workers better equipped to do skilled jobs.

### SOURCE 12

Victorian painting of a private 'dame school'. The 'dames' who ran such schools in their own homes were often little more than child-minders.

To try to raise standards while keeping down the rates, a system of 'Payment by Results' began in 1862. State grants to schools were based on tests taken by pupils. Joseph Ashby of Tysoe in Warwickshire here recalls such testing during his school days.

Two inspectors came once a year and carried out a dramatic examination … Each would sit at a desk and children would be called in turn to one or other. The master hovered round, calling children out as they were needed. The children could see … [his] vexation as a good pupil stuck at a word in the reading book he had been using all the year or sat motionless with his sum in front of him. The master's anxiety was deep for his earnings depended on the children's work….Right up the school…you did almost nothing except reading, writing and arithmetic.

W.E. Forster was the minister responsible for the 1870 Education Act. This is part of the speech he made in the House of Commons when introducing the Bill (February 1870).

Our object is to complete the present voluntary system, to fill up gaps, sparing the public money where it can be done without … We must not delay. Upon the speedy provision of elementary education depends our industrial prosperity. It is of no use trying to give technical teaching to our artisans without elementary education; uneducated labourers – and many of our labourers are utterly uneducated – are, for the most part, unskilled labourers.

An elementary school in Bristol in 1895. There are about 75 children and one teacher – who probably got the older pupils to help him teach the younger ones.

In 1861 less than half the $3\frac{1}{2}$ million children in England and Wales were reported to be attending school regularly. Of these, only a tenth learned the 'three Rs' properly. Reformers wanted schools to be provided in every community, paid for out of local rates. But householders naturally did not want the rates to go up (**Source 13**). The government was encouraged to come down on the side of the reformers after the 1867 Parliamentary Reform Act gave many working-class men the vote (see page 104). It was thought that voters should at least be able to read and write.

The turning point came with the Education Act of 1870. It allowed schools run by the church societies, which now numbered 20,000, to carry on as before with the help of larger government grants. Everywhere else, where proper schools were not provided, local School Boards were to be elected by ratepayers. These Boards could set up schools for five- to ten-year olds, paid for out of local rates and government grants. Parents were charged a small fee for each child, unless they were very poor (**Source 14**).

'Boards schools' were mostly drab and badly equipped, with eighty or ninety pupils to a class. The children themselves were often dirty and ragged with head-lice and skin diseases. Nevertheless it was from such beginnings that the 'state system' of education in England and Wales grew. By 1880 enough schools had been built to make attendance compulsory for all children up to 10 years old. The leaving age was raised to 12 by the end of the century. Meanwhile elementary (basic) education was made free to all in 1891.

## The education of women

In the elementary schools, working-class girls received much the same education as boys. But among the well-to-do, girls were given a very different education from their brothers. The boys were sent as boarders to expensive public schools such as Eton, Harrow and Rugby, from which many went on to university. Their sisters stayed at home and were usually taught reading, writing, music, painting and dancing by a private tutor called a governess. Girls were thought to need such 'accomplishments' in their search for a suitable husband; subjects such as arithmetic and science were for boys who would have to go out and earn their living.

A woman could not work and be considered a 'lady'. In well-to-do families women devoted their lives to leisure. They were like costly ornaments; the richness of their clothes and jewellery was evidence of the wealth of their menfolk. Such a way of life depended upon a ready supply of working-class girls to be domestic servants. There were far more women 'in service' than in any other job. However, many working-class women were also employed, on low wages, as dressmakers, laundrywomen and farm workers.

Some middle-class women rebelled against their boring, useless existence. Florence Nightingale defied her wealthy relatives to train as a nurse and look after sick and wounded soldiers in the Crimean War (1854–6). She later set up a school for nurses. Education was the key to improving women's lives. Two leading

**SOURCE 16**

Frances Buss had this to say about the education of girls when questioned by a government enquiry in 1865.

As to the instruction of the daughters of the middle class in London … I think that such education as they get is almost entirely showy and superficial; a little music, a little singing, a little French, a little ornaments work and nothing else, because many girls come to us who fancy they can speak French and play the piano, but have comparatively no knowledge of English or arithmetic.

**SOURCE 17**

Women university students studying science at Girton College, Cambridge, in 1905. Girton, founded in 1870, was the first women's college at either Cambridge or Oxford.

pioneers of girls' education were Frances Buss, who founded the North London Collegiate School in 1850, and Dorothea Beale who became principal of Cheltenham Ladies' College eight years later. Both set out to prepare girls for a career (**Source 16**).

Well schooled young women increasingly demanded the right to go to university. The first women's colleges at Cambridge and Oxford Universities were established in the 1870s. But although women students were allowed to sit the

SOURCE 18

Women telephonists operating the switchboard of the National Telephone Company, in about 1900.

examinations, it was many years before they were awarded degrees; the university authorities feared that these qualifications might be devalued if they were given to women! There were also women's colleges in London and the University there opened all its degree courses to women on equal terms with men in 1878.

Meanwhile women had to struggle to gain acceptance in respected professions such as the law and medicine. It was hard for them even to get a medical training until Elizabeth Garrett-Anderson, who had qualified in Paris, helped to establish the London School of Medicine for Women in 1874. Male doctors and patients of both sexes often refused to take women doctors seriously. It was said that single women had too little experience of life to practise medicine, while married women could not be expected to combine such demanding work with their domestic duties. In 1901 only 212 out of 22,000 doctors in England and Wales were women.

Elsewhere there were many new career opportunities for women. The growth of girls' education meant more women teachers were needed. As shops got bigger there was a demand for women shop assistants; many came from middle-class families in these years. Further job opportunities opened up for women with the coming of the typewriter in the 1870s. Census returns show that the number of women clerks in offices increased tenfold between 1881 and 1901. Meanwhile the first British telephone exchange opened in 1879 in London. In those days each call had to be put through by an operator; this was regarded as an ideal job for women.

## Women's rights

In 1877 a man stole a purse from Mrs Millicent Fawcett in a London railway station. He was caught and charged with 'stealing from the person of Millicent Fawcett a purse ... the property of Henry Fawcett (her husband)'. This made Millicent realise just how few rights she had as a married woman. A wife's money, property and even her children belonged to her husband. Both Millicent and her husband thought this unfair and campaigned for a change in the law. This came in 1882, when a Married Women's Property Act granted wives the right to own property and dispose of it as they wished. Four years later another Act forced a husband who had left his wife to pay towards her upkeep.

Such laws gave women new legal rights, yet women were still not entitled to vote in parliamentary elections. The first organised groups to campaign for female *suffrage* (voting rights) were the wives and daughters of Chartists, in the 1840s (see page 62). In 1869 one of the leading Victorian writers on politics, John Stuart Mill, published a book which argued strongly for women's suffrage (**Source 19**). Over the next 30 years the matter was debated in Parliament several times, but neither Liberal nor Conservative governments were in favour. Even the Queen was against what she called 'this mad, wicked folly of "Women's Rights"'.

A National Union of Women's Suffrage Societies was created in 1897 out of many small, local groups. Its first president was Millicent Fawcett. Public meetings were held and petitions organised. However in 1903 Emmeline Pankhurst, widow of a Liberal MP, decided that peaceful methods were not enough. She formed the Women's Social and Political Union (1903), a suffrage society determined to break the law if necessary to get women the vote. The battle of the 'Suffragettes' had begun. Women's struggle for equal rights and opportunities soon became one of the great issues of the twentieth century.

### SOURCE 19

This comes from J.S. Mill's book, *The Subjection of Women* (1869).

Under whatever conditions … men are admitted to the suffrage, there is not a shadow of justification for not admitting women under the same. The majority of the women of any class are not likely to differ in political opinion from the majority of the men of the same class, unless the question be one in which the interests of women, as such, are in some way involved; and if they are so, women require the suffrage as their guarantee of just and equal consideration.

### SOURCE 21

This *Punch* cartoon is entitled 'An Ugly Rush!' It shows 'John Bull' blocking the door to women's political rights.

### SOURCE 20

Millicent Fawcett (1847– 1929). Among those who inspired her to campaign for women's voting rights was her friend, John Stuart Mill.

# Assessment tasks

## A Knowledge and understanding

**1 a** Make a timeline to summarise some of the main social reforms of the 1800s which improved the lives of working-class people. In addition to public health and education, include reform of working conditions in factories and mines (see pages 41 and 54).

**b** Can you explain why, despite such reforms, up to a third of town-dwellers were found to be living in conditions of extreme poverty at the end of the century?

**2** Why was faster progress made on improving public health standards (e.g. sewerage, street cleansing and water supply) than standards of working-class housing in the nineteenth century?

**3** What ideas and attitudes had to be overcome before women could
**a** own property?
**b** have the same educational opportunities as their brothers?
**c** choose to follow a professional career?
**d** vote in parliamentary elections?

## B Interpretations and sources

**4** Here two historians consider the main motive behind the 1870 Education Act.

It was the Reform Bill of 1867 which gave the first real impetus (spur) to the creation of a national system of free and compulsory education...A wider franchise (more people with voting rights) demanded a better educated electorate...The Education Act of 1870 set up locally-elected school boards which could compel attendance.
(David Thomson, 1950)

It has sometimes been suggested that this (the desire to educate the new voters) was a motive for passing the Education Act of 1870...There are two other much more likely reasons: one, a genuine concern at the ignorance of the nation's children, which it was thought led to immorality and crime; the other the belief that an efficient workforce must be educated.
(Mary Lazarus, 1969)

**a** How is it possible for two historians to come to such different conclusions? What does this tell you about the nature of history?
**b** Could they *both* be right? Give reasons for your answer.

**5** Re-read Sources 9 and 14.
**a** What reasons are put forward for reforming (i) public health, and (ii) elementary education?
**b** What do these sources tell you about government attitudes towards (i) dirt and squalor, and (ii) ignorance?

**6** Look carefully at Source 20.
**a** What does 'John Bull' represent?
**b** What does the cartoon's title and the way women are drawn tell you about the artist's attitude to the subject?
**c** What suggestion is there that women are not united on this issue?

# Index

Topics in the National Curriculum Orders are in bold type.
Page numbers in *italics* refer to illustrations.